the Beagle and his Boy

Cathy Cook

Amethyst Fire Publishing

Amethyst Fire Publishing, PO Box 1018, Concord, NC 28026

Copyright © 2018 Cathy Cook

All rights reserved. No part of this book may be reproduced, scanned, or distributed in any printed or electronic form without permission of the author.

Library of Congress Cataloging-in-Publication Data is available.

ISBN 978-1-7327792-0-4

Artist Credit: Paige Miles
Cover Credit: Anne Davis-Groebner

This work is a true story and shared by the best recollection of the author. Most names of individuals and institutions are omitted, and some minor narrative details are fictitious or omitted, for reasons of privacy.

For Jessica

Love saves us all.

Part I

Life

Prologue

The cotton-candy sky is what I always notice first.

Silver clouds drift quickly, trailing purple wisps in every direction. If I study the cumulus artists' works, I sight a dragon. Then its wings lift to a butterfly's flight before the empty cocoon morphs into a ship, the once-wings now billowing sails on a turbulent sea.

I'm mesmerized with cloud art, but I know the sky's canvas is merely teasing me. Lowering my eyes to a scene I know well, I still cannot help but gasp at the earth's beauty. Azure grass, soft as velvet, spreads beneath my bare feet. Poplar, red bud, oak, maple trees shed multi-colored leaves, gently cascading. Distant majestic mountains soar to the clouds.

And from the other side of the nearest foothill, I hear them before I see them. The boy's laughter peals through the air like sleigh bells and ancient cathedral chimes joined in medley. With a call-and-response cadence, the hound's gentle yaps float alongside the boy's joyous chorus.

I catch a glimpse of their game of tag as they run over the hill's crest. They pause for only a second before our eyes meet, and then – this is the moment I treasure most – they see me and begin to run to me.

Laughing and barking still, the boy's arms outstretched, his strong legs carrying him swiftly; the pup wagging, leaping, keeping pace beside the boy. They run closer and closer and closer until my aching, reaching fingers almost touch them.

Then, as every other time, my body jerks and I awake from the dream.

Chapter 1: Expectations

I don't know anything about the dog who gave birth to Jack. I don't know her name, her stature, or her markings. I don't know her medical history or food preferences. I don't know her bloodline, or her partner's lineage.

From Jack's inner strength and his loving nature, I don't find it impossible to think of his parents as noble hounds. Perhaps his mom came from a long line of dogs who were faithful, gentle, and loving companions to their human friends. She could have been the hero hound of adventure stories told around campfires. Maybe the male who sired him had pedigrees and a string of fancy names.

I have no information about the circumstances of Jack's birth. I pray he was born in a cozy, dry, warm room where his momma was pampered by humans who loved her and her puppies. I hope he snuggled with siblings before he could open his eyes to see the world around him. I want to believe he smelled the good food shared with his mom, and nuzzled at her teats for plenty himself.

I don't know anything about Jack's life as a puppy. I dream he rolled and ran and fell over and nipped and played with happy pup sisters and brothers. I hope he gently weaned away from his mom's milk to an abundance of healthy food and clean water. I long to know he had a warm, soft bed on which to sleep and a safe place to play through the days.

No, I don't know one detail of how Jack's life began, but I do know he soon would live a life no dog deserves.

The lamb had a real bell around its neck, tied with a yellow satin ribbon. I picked up the plump animal with its fluffy fake fur, also yellow, and the sound of the bell made me smile. The toy had no battery compartment, so the creature didn't nod its head, walk, or even "Baaaaa." To me, that lamb seemed peaceful and content – the perfect first toy for my first child.

Only half an hour before, I'd waited on hold while my doctor's office pulled up the results from the test taken two days earlier. Yes, I was pregnant. Muttering "See y'all later" to my coworkers without a word about my news, I walked to the downtown shop only a block away. Musty racks of women's clothing crowded the store's front displays, but a back room featured tiny dresses and miniature suits for newborns, toddlers, and young children. I fingered delicate outfits and noticed fancy play clothes that likely would never see a mud puddle or the view from the top of trees. The store's wares weren't in my preferred style or price range, but today was a special occasion. I spotted a small section with toys overshadowed by that lamb and knew the fuzzy toy would go home with me in celebration.

I paid for the lamb, awkwardly cradling it while counting out my money, and carried it out of the store without a bag. Walking from the shop to my car in the rear parking lot of my workplace, I giggled every time its bell jingled.

I know about Jack's young adult life through the eyes of his neighbor. The kitchen window over her sink looked out to the remote edge of the property next door. From her viewpoint there, she didn't see the neighbor's house on the hill, but had a clear view of the bottom of their sloped yard. Out her kitchen window, she saw the stake driven into the ground, the chain attached to the stake, the metal bucket a few feet away, and a small plastic structure.

And she saw the beagle. She watched him day after day as he paced and jumped and struggled against the 20 feet of heavy chain that shackled him to the stake. Chained far away from the house, he spent every day and night apart from human contact. She listened to him whimpering and barking, as he tried to call to the family who'd abandoned him there, begging for their attention. Each time he heard a noise from the direction of the house, he reared up on his back legs and strained to be free.

The beagle's neighbor noted his barren surroundings with no bedding or blankets. Sometimes a person from the house would come down the hill to hurl meager discarded table scraps or to dump water into the five-gallon bucket, but not often enough to ensure he had enough food or clean water. A small rectangular enclosure made of flimsy plastic provided no useful protection for the thin pup.

The chain bound the dog to the stake through every type of weather. He stood shivering, unprotected in snow and ice. He lay flat on the parched ground, panting, through oppressive heat and humidity in the summer. Worst of all, he cowered as low as he could make himself during storms of booming thunder, streaks of lightning, and torrential rains.

She noticed the hound limping and knew he must have some type of injury, but she didn't see any care or medical attention given to him. Once when she knew the neighbors were gone, she moved as close as she dared to the edge of her yard at the property line. She saw the beagle's right foot bent under as if it had been broken.

The kind neighbor tried her best to get help as months passed. She repeatedly called animal control, but the county where she and the beagle resided required only evidence of food, water, and shelter. The beagle had the bucket, a plate, and the plastic house that made bad conditions even worse. The authorities said nothing could be done.

She washed her dishes and watched through tears of frustration.

I drove home with the toy lamb in the front passenger seat, carried it inside and upstairs, and placed it on the floor in the middle of the small, empty room across from my bedroom. There, the lamb stood stoically while I transformed its surroundings into a nursery. New paint on the walls changed their color from dull beige to a pastel yellow with bright white trim. A delivery crew placed the new oak crib, a matching dresser with a pad to use as a changing table, and handmade bumper pads and quilt. Stripped of its peeling paint, a second-hand rocker became a sunny yellow corner chair. Soon the yellow lamb moved from the floor to the rocker's seat, and I smiled at it whenever passing by the nursery.

As the spare room changed to be ready for my baby's arrival, I experienced my own transformation. In an appointment with my doctor soon after my pregnancy test, she proclaimed me 10 weeks along. Her office sent me home with prenatal vitamins and an estimated due date in mid-March. For the first weeks of pregnancy, breakfast consisted of plain saltine crackers or dry toast due to morning nausea, but soon I had my appetite back and felt great.

And hungry! Soon after my first trimester checkup, I attended a business lunch at a favorite local restaurant where the servers brought out their dessert specialty, hot fudge cake. The warm treat featured a slab of moist chocolate cake, topped with vanilla ice cream, another piece of chocolate cake, and warm hot fudge flowing down all of the layers. For the rest of my pregnancy, I craved that delicious dessert. Everyone assured me I was "eating for two," and at each visit back to that restaurant, my favorite server insisted, "Your baby's hungry for cake today!"

Baby showers, one with family and another with coworkers, filled the nursery's small dresser with bibs, diapers, and infant-sized play clothes appropriate for either a girl or a boy. My grandmother made a beautiful yellow crocheted quilt; as I opened it, she apologized for an error in stitches she'd tried to repair, but I never saw anything but perfection and love. A church friend knitted another small, handmade baby blanket, and a coworker sewed a colorful pillow for the rocking chair. My next-door neighbor brought a yellow plastic rattle that made a small, delicate rattling sound when shaken.

Determined to be as well prepared as possible for motherhood, I read volumes by experts on baby care and child rearing. My nightstand held magazines offering information about breast feeding, developmental stages, and teething. The book with which I spent the biggest amount of time was called "10,000 Baby Names." Despite hours poring over the names and thinking about every ancestor's name in the family genealogy, no name seemed right for me to give either a daughter or a son. I spent lots of time thumbing through the book, saying girls' and boys' names aloud to see how they sounded, and still couldn't decide.

At the beginning of my third trimester, a six-week session of Lamaze classes began at the local hospital. New parents-to-be met for two hours each Monday night. At my first class, the instructor focused on her credentials, our introductions to one another, and a tour of the hospital's maternity floor. During the third week when she showed a film featuring a woman actually giving birth, I closed my eyes and sang happy songs in my head. Back home between classes, I regularly practiced the different types of breathing techniques. "Hee hee hee hoo. Hee hee hee hoo."

At the end of the fourth week's class, my Lamaze instructor said we moms should choose a focal object for use during the birthing process, anything to divert our attention away from the pain and focus us on childbirth's joy. That night I walked through the house, looking around at my belongings. The yellow lamb? He was a little too large and seemed happier sitting atop his pillow on the rocking chair waiting for the new baby. An onyx ring my parents gave me to celebrate high school graduation? No, the instructor had cautioned against jewelry at the hospital.

Finally I chose a sea shell I'd picked up on my last visit to the beach. Since childhood, the ocean always brought me more inspiration and peace than any other destination. My parents first dipped my toes in ocean waves before I was even a year old. Our family traveled to the coast for the week of July 4th almost every year of my childhood. A high school graduation ritual took me to the beach with friends for my first trip without parents. With college classmates, I escaped exams and term papers beside the ocean. And to this day, whenever I want to dream on paper or to write an article or book, I head to the shore.

Over the years I'd collected many shells, but that evening I felt drawn to a small, spherical shell with the jagged crack at its opening. My collection once included only shells that seemed perfect, but in the past years I appreciated the strength and beauty of those with broken pieces or exteriors worn from the elements. When I chose that shell for my hospital suitcase stack, I selected it because it was a beautiful, peaceful treasure small enough to hold in my hand.

I didn't know until years later it was called an olive shell.

Chapter 2: Homecoming

Graduation day from Lamaze classes came in January, two months before my baby's due date. I left work early that afternoon, carefully stepping around a few icy patches in the parking lot from a snow storm several days before. Back home, a quick supper allowed time for changing out of my too-tight maternity dress. I felt almost giddy with excitement at the thought of my last class. The nursery was ready, baby showers were over, and now I'd graduate from Lamaze in plenty of time to launder and put away the new diapers before the baby came.

As I started to pull on my comfy pregnancy jeans, the sight of blood startled me. Trembling fingers dialed the after-hours emergency number for my obstetrician. An on-call doctor asked me a few questions. No pain, I told him. No other symptoms. Yes, bright red blood and not just a few drops.

The doctor told me to come immediately to the emergency room of the nearest hospital. I hurriedly left the house, forgetting to take my already carefully packed suitcase with the new baby's coming home outfit.

When I rushed past the nursery door, the lamb watched me leave.

Twelve miles stretched between my house and the hospital. Halfway there, my lower abdomen and back began to ache with a heaviness matched by my heart. I tried to stifle the fear, longing to rewind the clock an hour earlier, and go to my class. I wanted to have my baby in the way the Lamaze teacher described: gentle music, focused breath, beach imagery, and the presence of loving family and friends to welcome my little girl or boy into the world.

Fear rose as the stabbing pains intensified. I began to hum the song so often sung to my baby in the womb. "You are my sunshine, my only sunshine…" I wanted to sing the words bravely, but knew something felt horribly wrong.

I remember thinking the baby and I both could die.

The hound's neighbor walked into her kitchen and over to her sink to rinse out a glass. As much as her heart hurt when she looked, she automatically raised her eyes each time to the dog at the end of the chain. She loathed that chain. The poor beagle was limping, moving awkwardly as he always did now. He seemed thinner than ever before.

She and the beagle heard the loud noise at the same time, probably the garbage truck making its weekly collections on their street. The dog startled, and then began to beg and bark. He struggled to be free, raised himself as best he could with his injuries, and leaned with all his might against the burdensome linked metal.

The beagle lifted his head, howling his hound plea to the wind.

In the house next door, the desperate neighbor raised her own face to the heavens and shouted aloud, stomping her foot against the kitchen floor in protest. "God, do something!"

At that moment, the chain broke.

When I awoke in my hospital room the morning of my baby's birth, I first noticed drab green walls and the dryness of my mouth. I closed my eyes and drifted back into darkness. When next I awoke, a doctor making rounds gently told me I had a baby boy, but needed to sleep before we talked more about the birth. I woke again a short time later, aggravated by IV tubes and extreme itching that turned out to be a reaction to morphine. Even more aggravating was the nurse who told me I'd needed two units of blood, but refused to say anything about my baby, only promising she'd page the doctor on call.

On the morning of the third day, I first heard the account of events that happened after I lost consciousness in the hospital's birthing center. My son's Apgar score at birth registered zero. A pediatrician resuscitated my little boy, and an ambulance transported him to a neonatal intensive care unit of a hospital in the larger city next to ours.

Apgar? Oh yes, my Lamaze teacher taught our class about Apgar scores as the indicator of a newborn's health.

"Zero?" I asked, and the doctor confirmed.

Dead on arrival, I kept thinking.

"Do you have any questions?" asked the doctor who told me the story.

"Will he be okay?" I whispered.

The doctor's hesitation gave me the answer I didn't want. "Your baby's condition is critical," he answered, patting my arm.

I posed only one more question: "When can I hold my baby?"

The neighbor dashed through her kitchen, down the stairs, and to her basement's exterior door. She flung open the door, saw the dog running, and yelled "Here! Here!" She felt afraid he'd be terrified of people and flee in the opposite direction.

Instead, at the sound of her pleading voice, the pup turned to run straight toward her, past her, through the door, and inside her home. She slammed the door shut behind her.

Finally, the beagle was safe.

He was safe, but in an appalling condition. Due to the neglect and abuse of the family next door, the poor dog was malnourished and underweight. He wore no rabies vaccination tag, and he'd never been neutered. One leg dangled as if it were broken, and that foot's dew claws had grown into the flesh above his paws. He had bleeding open wounds and suffered obvious pain.

The beagle's neighbor followed the letter of the law regarding stray dogs. The volunteer who answered her telephone call to the county's animal control explained she must keep any found dog for three days and make an effort to try finding its owner before claiming it for herself. The beagle's neighbor put an ad in the newspaper with the dog's general description and with her phone number. She gave thanks for each day without an answer to the advertisement and with no "Lost" signs posted in her neighborhood.

When the hound began to bark or howl, she took him for rides in her car so the neighbors wouldn't hear. The days dragged by as she listened for the dreaded doorbell or phone call. Finally, the required number of days passed, and she drove her furry friend to the nearby rescue where she surrendered him.

The neighbor wanted to keep him, to care for him always, but she couldn't afford another dog, and she couldn't move from her home beside the neighbors who'd abused him. She cried as she gave up the beagle, but knew her loss was an act of love. Out of her love, she surrendered him.

The first sight of my baby terrified me.

Only a few hours after an ambulance transported me between hospitals and admissions placed me in a room, a doctor acquiesced to my begging for the chance to see my son. A nurse wheeled me down the hallway of the maternity floor. The doors to every room held congratulatory signs and bows for mothers who'd given birth. My door was empty. My wheelchair ride passed moms holding their newborn infants. My arms felt heavy and lonely.

As the nurse pushed me close to an entrance for the Neonatal Intensive Care Unit, I saw the bright yellow sign warning about all of the precautions. Another nurse came through the double doors, greeted me, and helped me put on a gown, gloves, and mask. She wheeled me into the space and past the tiniest baby I'd ever seen. Later that week the baby's dad told me she'd been there for three months and still weighed only two pounds.

All of the unit's babies lay in individual beds, rectangular-shaped with clear sides; the beds were built into what seemed to be monitored carts on wheels. Some babies cried as they lifted an arm or leg. Others were eerily still. An alarming cacophony of instruments beeped, buzzed, and sometimes screamed their warnings. I choked on the smell of medicine and sterility and sickness.

Moving through that unit, my fear grew with each infant we passed. I remember thinking of the months I'd spent preparing for this moment when I'd see my baby for the first time. I created his sunny yellow room, talked and sang to him, felt him kick and stretch. I expected my baby to come into the world in a joyous way – to see him and hold him at birth, and to cherish forever my memory of the first time I saw his face. I expected the birth every pregnant mom expects. I wondered if people understand the deeper meaning when they lightly say, "I don't care if it's a boy or a girl, as long as it's healthy."

The nurse guided my wheelchair in front of a medical station in the far corner, leaned over to snap on the chair's brakes, and lightly said, "Here's your boy!" She helped me stand beside the bed, and I raised my eyes to see my baby. At first I noticed his features: the gaunt face and body, fragile limbs, and closed eyes. His head looked as sharply angular as an almond. He didn't move.

Then I saw the wires and cords that ran to machines breathing for him, feeding him, monitoring his body's distress, keeping him alive. His face had tubing taped to his nose and mouth. Soft gauze-like material looped around his wrists to keep him from flailing and scratching himself with the sharp nails on his miniscule fingers. Rolled white cloths stretched alongside his body to support his position. A tiny piece of cloth covered his private parts. White tape and IV needles and wires from monitors covered his body. I diverted my eyes and saw the chart posting his vital signs where a nurse recorded his weight was down to only three pounds.

I felt as if I would faint. I couldn't seem to catch my breath, and wondered if I could keep from throwing up. The nurse touched my shoulder and asked if I were okay. I managed only a slight nod. The nurse gently told me I couldn't hold him yet, but that it would be wonderful to talk to him.

I cleared my throat, trying to speak but instead choking back a sob. I looked again at his tiny face where he'd opened dark eyes. I swallowed hard, took some deep breaths, and then opened my mouth and said the only words I knew were true at that moment.

"I love you, Christopher."

I fell in love with the beagle at first sight.

On the day I met the lemon-colored pup, I'd arrived early on a Sunday morning to prepare for a community "Blessing of the Animals" service at the local rescue organization's building. I greeted the volunteers and staff before setting up equipment and props. As people and their animal companions arrived, I recognized some from previous Blessing events and knew that others were attending for their first time.

The short worship service began with scripture from Genesis about our human responsibilities as stewards of all creation. We prayed for creatures, both furry and not, who needed rescuing. Then I began my favorite part of any Blessing event: meeting each dog and cat who'd accompanied their human, and blessing each one with the sign of a heart on their furry heads (or in the air above them if they preferred) and the words, "You are loved!"

After the worship event, I continued the Blessings by walking throughout the facility to see all of the rescue's occupants awaiting their forever homes. The front hall of the building held individual glass enclosures for cats. Stopping at each kitty, I read aloud the name printed on a card and spoke words of love. Another room featured a large open space with glass walls where over twenty cats played, climbed, or napped in the sunshine. Sweet kitties ran to greet me.

After blessing each of the cats, I headed to the dogs' living quarters. Pups, some in pairs and some alone, were housed in bright, happy cubicles. Volunteers spoke to me as they passed with dogs who couldn't wait to play outside or walk the nearby trails. I called out the dogs' names and uttered a blessing. Sometimes my heart hurt when I saw dogs known from previous visits, creatures who were spending too long in even this loving place. I lifted prayers for the perfect home soon to come for each creature there.

By the time my full round for blessings ended, I felt exhausted, emotionally and physically. My admiration for staff and volunteers in rescue work multiplied tenfold on each of my visits.

The rescue's director approached me as I returned to the lobby prior to leaving for the day.

"We have a dog whose leg was amputated a few days ago. Will you please give him a special blessing?"

She opened the door to a small back office. As soon as I stepped in, a beagle with three legs began to hop toward me.

I knelt before the pup, and the director began to tell me the dog's story. She first met the beagle when he was surrendered, took one look, and knew he needed special attention. Immediately the dog began to get the care he needed. Staff provided good quality food and fresh, plentiful water. His indoor lodging, heated or cooled as needed, included an outdoor run. The veterinarian on staff tested for any signs of disease, gave his vaccinations, scheduled him to be neutered, and treated his flesh wounds. The beagle's health was stable.

Yet his front right leg, broken and then ignored, could not be repaired. For too long, he'd walked with his entire foot curled under. The rescue's veterinarian had no choice but to amputate his leg.

After surgery, the beagle spent his recovery in a small private office with his own crate, cozy with bedding. Strong medicines almost kept his pain under control, but staff still heard him whimpering between doses. One volunteer brought his first gift: a soft yellow squeaker toy shaped like a banana.

While the director spoke, I slowly offered my hand for the dog to sniff with his long beagle snout. He put his nose against my arm. I noticed his long, white eyelashes and soulful eyes. Bandages still covered his front shoulder area where the leg had been amputated. His body was lean, still too thin, but muscular. I spoke softly to him and his thick, straight tail moved in a slight wag. The end of his tail looked just like a paintbrush tipped in white paint. As he moved his body closer, I slowly reached out and stroked his neck. His fur there surprised me with its silky softness.

My eyes met the beagle's eyes once again and only then did I see the mark on his forehead: a white heart.

I turned to the director and said, "I want to adopt him."

My application for his adoption was completed and filed that very day. Due to his need to recover from the amputation surgery, the beagle could not leave the rescue facility for several weeks. I bought a new collar and leash, notified our vet's office to set up an initial appointment date, prepared a crate with bedding, and bought a small supply of the food he'd been eating at the shelter to transition his diet. I decided to name him "Captain Jack," after my favorite pirate.

When finally the approved day came, I excitedly arrived at the rescue, signed the papers, and paid the adoption fee. A staff member handed me a copy of his vaccination papers and a bag she said held a toy given to Jack by one of the volunteers. "He loves that toy," she emphasized.

Jack came out to greet me as soon as someone opened the door of the office housing his crate, but then he retreated. He obviously did not want to leave the safety of his small room, and quickly went back into his crate. Staff helped coax him out into the lobby, but he resisted leaving the building and had to be carried out to the car. He repeatedly tried to turn back. He certainly didn't want to get into any stranger's car. When the rescue's staff took a photograph of us leaving the parking lot, the photo showed me smiling and holding my arms around a beagle who looked terrified.

On Mother's Day, Jack came home with me, bringing the only possession he'd ever owned: his yellow banana toy.

I stayed as a patient in the hospital for a week, visiting Christopher at every opportunity. Through those visits, I never grew comfortable seeing him with IV needles protruding from his little feet, or the machines around him monitoring his vital signs. Every doctor's report during the first few days was the same: "He's not out of the woods yet." "I can't promise you anything." "He's struggling." Each time a medical professional walked into my room with too solemn a face, I'd try to brace myself for the news.

Yet by the end of that week, I began to observe the smallest positive changes. Christopher graduated to wearing a tiny diaper that the nurse explained was sized for premature babies. He donned a soft yellow toboggan, a gift from volunteers who knitted them for premie babies to help retain body heat. His bed looked happier with the addition of a Snoopy no larger than my palm nestled next to him. And finally on the day before my discharge, his doctors stopped beginning their reports to me with the warning, "Still life and death situation – no promises."

The morning of my discharge, I held my son for the first time. The attending nurse nodded her approval of the required gown over my clothes and the usual washing of my hands and arms with disinfecting soap, but then allowed me to remove my mask and gloves. Staff placed a large wooden rocking chair near Christopher's incubator, while the nurse unhooked some of the wires attached to my tiny baby. I confessed my fear of hurting him to his nurse, but she assured me we'd both be fine. She swaddled him in a white hospital blanket, and gingerly placed him in my arms.

I rocked my baby boy, sang to him, and told him about the room awaiting him at home. We rocked and rocked until the nurse came to tell me he needed to rest.

Christopher had to stay as a patient for eight more weeks after my discharge. I traveled the 25 miles to see him as often as possible, and called every day for a progress report. Hospital staff answered my questions and telephoned with updates. On some visits, I met other parents who were traveling to see their babies. Some babies never had visitors, the nurses admitted when asked.

His doctors scheduled several consultations with me during Christopher's stay. For the first few weeks, the doctors continued to caution me about possible critical setbacks. After he was more stable, the doctors' conversations changed. I recall one doctor's conference more than any others. After asking me to sit across from his desk in a private office, the doctor said he wanted to talk about Christopher's prognosis. He spoke about the lack of oxygen during the birth process, resulting in lasting damage to the brain. He said words like "retardation," "seizures," and "cerebral palsy." I listened without speaking, nodding my head to let him know I heard what he said. He gave examples of things Christopher might never do, including talking and walking. Then he began to tell me about some residential options for Christopher's care after he could leave the hospital but I interrupted then, saying I already knew my child would go home with me as soon as he safely could be released.

Years later I read the doctor's notes from that conversation. "The mother does not understand," he wrote, "Despite my insistence on the severity of her son's future limitations, she doesn't understand."

He was wrong. I understood every word he said and some he didn't say.

Two more months passed before Christopher's condition was stable enough to transfer him from the Neonatal Intensive Care Unit and back to the local hospital. With my son then only minutes away, I visited every day, often during his feeding times with bottles holding only two ounces. The nursing staff taught me to feed him by his nasal-esophageal tube because he still was not strong enough to take enough nourishment from a bottle. Ten days later and three months after his birth, Christopher finally came home to his sunny room where his yellow lamb sat waiting.

Chapter 3: Brave and Strong

I never knew a three-legged dog before Jack.

When the call came from the rescue's director saying Jack's surgical wounds had healed enough for me to bring him home, I began to worry. Any self-confidence in my abilities to welcome new rescue animals vanished at the thought of Jack's missing leg. My bookcases held stacks of experts' books about introducing rescue dogs and cats to new settings and to other pets. Previous training taught me how to housetrain a dog, how to transition them to a healthy diet, and how to help them enjoy spending quiet time in a crate when left home alone. Dogs and cats always taught me new lessons, but usually any issues could be resolved with a little patience and lots of love.

But how could I help this beagle live with only three legs? The attending veterinary surgeon warned of the challenges for the amputation of a front leg. The rescue's staff said Jack continued to heal well, but cautioned about the problems of adjusting to any new place. Already a gate blocked the stairway to upstairs, and non-slip rugs covered slippery floors. But could he even move from one room to another? Would he be able to manage steps into the house? Did he need a ramp from the backyard deck onto the grass? How did a three-legged dog play? Or potty?

On the day Jack came home, I'd taken great care to make certain the house seemed as peaceful as possible. No people or pets would be present until he had some time to settle into his new environment. Family and friends, excited about Jack's arrival, agreed to wait a while to meet him. My two dogs and two cats were confined to other spaces in the house so Jack could meet them later too.

After an uneventful drive, we finally arrived home. When the car's engine shut off, Jack awoke from fitful sleep and nervously waited for me to unhook his seatbelt tether. I led him down a ramp from car to driveway, and slowly, carefully walked with him from the car to the house. We moved with apprehensive deliberation, his leash loose, but close to me. Jack panted with anxiety, while I tried not to hold my breath.

When he reached the two steps from the garage to the kitchen entry, Jack hesitated. "Can you do it, sweet boy?" Jack's body trembled, but he managed to move up the stairs without falling. As soon as we reached the kitchen, I knelt down to remove the leash attached to Jack's new collar, expecting him to flatten out on the floor and need to be coaxed farther into the house.

"You're home, sweet beagle," I said gently.

The sound of my voice and the word, "home," triggered greetings from one of Jack's new fur brothers. Despite my careful plans and attempt to sneak in quietly, Patches, the guardian of the pack, heard our entrance even from an upstairs room and answered with an exuberant "Yay! You're home!" series of barks.

Of course Jack heard the barks and responded with his own yap.

Immediately Jack took off! He ran through the kitchen, past the dining room table, and then – before I could reach him or utter a syllable of the terror felt – he leaped and soared over the back of the living room couch. How did he jump so high? And how did he not fall off the couch? Somehow he miraculously stopped on the seat portion and then calmly hopped down onto the floor, looking up at me as if to say, "See what three-legged beagles can do?"

Jack's dramatic entry that first day foreshadowed a long adjustment period even more challenging than I had feared, but not for any of the reasons imagined. While his physical wounds healed nicely, the invisible wounds were far more significant. In fact, Jack's amputation did not deter him from any activity, but his traumatic past caused problems with every aspect of his new life.

Inside the house, my new pup initially wanted to stay in small spaces where he felt safer. At first, he slept on cozy bedding inside a crate placed in the laundry room, a room similar in size to the one where he'd slept at the rescue. Jack spent some time in his crate, but seemed even more comfortable hiding in my clothes closet beneath the hanging skirts or in the pantry behind a case of water.

From the start, he was shy with people, but friendly as long as the humans were coming into the spaces he'd adopted as his safety zones. He'd greet visitors with a wag of his paint-brush tail. In only a few days, Jack gradually began to take tentative steps into the larger spaces of the house. He came to the kitchen for mealtimes and the living room during the evening.

Despite his initial fears of the house's larger spaces, noises, and new people he met, especially men, Jack wasn't afraid of any animal. Over the next few weeks, Jack befriended the other rescued furry members of the household: Patches, Oz, Dodger, and Raja. Patches was the pack leader, an intelligent and serious border collie mix, in his early teens. Ozzie was my protective lap dog, a black and gray terrier mix who reminded me of Toto in my favorite movie, "The Wizard of Oz." Dodger, who confidently presided over all the dogs, was a huge, gray cat in his early twenties, the only cat I've ever met who liked to play fetch with a stick. Raja, a beautiful and shy calico, enjoyed her solitude upstairs, but occasionally her curiosity led her to creep downstairs and watch the others' antics from any high perch.

As soon as he showed signs of feeling more secure, Jack began spending his nights in my bedroom with the rest of the furry family members. At first he slept in his crate, resting as comfortably as he had in the laundry room, while furry siblings dozed around him – the oldest dog, Patches, on the floor near the door in his preferred guarding function, Ozzie on the end of the bed with his head beside my leg, and the cats curled on the window seat.

After a couple of weeks, I placed a comfortable dog bed with a freshly-washed quilt on the floor beside my own bed and left open his crate's door. On the very first night with the new bed in place, Jack bounced out of his crate and right into that bed. Every night after, he slept there beside me. I could drop my arm off my bed's side and touch him.

Meal times gave me other clues of Jack's previous neglect. With usual beagle gusto, he enjoyed eating anything and everything given. Initially meals meant kibble and treats fed by hand to keep him from gulping his food too quickly and to make him more comfortable with human nurturing. If another pup came too close to his food bowl, even an empty bowl, Jack growled menacingly. I moved his meals into a separate area, hoping he'd feel confident about always having enough to eat without having to share.

Later his food issues were evident in other problem behaviors. Jack's time outdoors required careful monitoring because he began to eat sticks, plants, or sometimes even dirt. A trainer friend described Jack as an example of a "garbage can dog," a pup that's not had enough to eat so later continues to forage for anything. Even though Jack now consumed plenty of a good quality food, supplements, and healthy treats of carrots, green beans, pumpkin, and the occasional "cookies," he continued to try to eat dirt.

Ozzie always tested any animal who came into the house, and a friendly three-legged beagle was no exception. As my self-appointed protector and lap dog extraordinaire, Ozzie always reacted when a new-to-the-household creature approached his post. Little Ozzie would fly off of my lap in a ferocious fit, never biting but fiercely chasing the newcomer away. Jack seemed too afraid of laps or even people at first, so he and Ozzie quickly made peace and later became best friends.

While inside the house, Jack adjusted fairly quickly to his newfound freedom of movement and of being with others. Yet he remained terrified of the outside. It was as if, once he fled from being chained to the scary outside world, he vowed never to go outside again. That fear made his toilet times challenging. I proceeded first with standard crate use for his toilet training, but he didn't want to step through any exterior door. Even on a leash, he'd move with me to the back door, but then try to turn around. He refused to walk through the door on his own, even with the other dogs running out to play or do their business.

For the first few weeks, my terrified beagle went outside only when someone carried him. Then Jack would tremble and cower – and not go to the toilet! Back inside, he'd potty right on the living room carpet. His fears made it difficult but finally, after a few months, he began to run outside just long enough to potty and then he'd dash right back inside. Soon after, wood floors replaced that smelly, stained carpet.

Over time, the routine movements of the other dogs helped Jack's transition to spending some time in the yard. They'd stand at the door, ringing the bells hanging from the doorknob to alert me they wanted to go outside. As I approached the door to open it, they'd wag and even bark in anticipation. Jack's pack would be so excited to run outside the back door for play and potty, he'd almost run out with them – but two steps onto the porch, he'd realize he was outside and turn back around.

Gradually, over months, he would dash outside with them and then stay for a while to follow them around the yard. Patches would lead the pup brigade from the deck's steps to the fence line and then all around the perimeter of the yard. By the end of his first year after adoption, Jack was running outside with the other dogs.

Jack had no difficulty keeping up with his canine siblings, and he quickly joined into their daily routines. He seemed to look up to Patches, following him around as if Patches were the cool kid at school. Patches ignored Jack's adoration, but didn't mind when Jack shadowed him around the yard. Ozzie soon bowed in play postures to nudge Jack into running after him. Dodger never moved quickly around any of the dogs, wisely sauntering past them. Only Raja hid from Jack. Although she didn't mind the other dogs, she startled at the sight and sound of Jack's awkward "hopping" movement from his three-legged gait.

While Jack grew slightly more confident outside, he still startled easily. If he heard any unexpected or loud sound, if a car back-fired or a neighbor cranked their mower, he'd flee back inside. The week when the neighbors put on a new roof was agonizing because he would go outside and, as soon as someone hammered, he'd dash back to the house, trembling from nose to tail.

Some of Jack's fears didn't show up until months after his homecoming. I cried when I once too quickly reached for a book on the bookcase over my head, also over Jack's body, and he dropped to the floor, cowering in terror, as if I'd hit him. He remained afraid if ever a person lifted a hand over him. He also seemed much more cautious around men than women. At times, he would exhibit anxiety over the humans leaving the house, even though he rested securely in his crate with happy music playing nearby.

Out of all Jack's fears, the worst was his fear of thunderstorms. As soon as he would sense a storm coming, he would begin to try to hide his entire body under a table or inside a closet. By the time thunder could be heard or lightning flashes seen, Jack already had started his desperate attempts to run away from the storm. He'd frantically bolt from room to room. Sometimes he'd try to flee up the front stairway, much to my distress, because he could have easily slipped on those steps. The sturdy gate blocking the bottom of the stairs couldn't stop him when he panicked. He'd nudge past the gate's corners, or even knock down the gate by jumping against it, just so he could run up to the landing. When he finally felt as if he'd reached a safer place, usually with his whole body stretched flat beneath the lower-hanging clothes in a closet, he'd stay there for hours until he was convinced the storm had passed.

His fright from thunderstorms transferred to anything with similar conditions. The flash from my camera sent Jack scurrying to find shelter when I first tried to take his photograph. He spent an hour trembling in his crate after a faltering light bulb flickered. The neighbor's fireworks for their annual July 4th gathering kept him trembling in the back of my closet for the rest of the night.

No matter what the terrors of each day or night brought, Jack somehow had the courage to face the next new situation. Despite his tragic past with abusive treatments by humans who never deserved him, Jack never gave up on loving people. He taught me the meaning of bravery – not as the absence of fear, but as the persistence to live and love regardless of fear. Whenever Jack lay trembling, I held him close, repeating this mantra over and over: "Jack, you're a beagle, brave and strong."

"Stay strong," I murmured to myself, despite feeling exhausted and weak. "You're tough and he's tough," I insisted aloud while holding my baby at 3 a.m., trying to coax him to drink a few drops. "You can do this!" I whispered after walking out of the pediatrician's office where the doctor warned about my infant's failure to thrive.

The celebratory mood from Christopher's homecoming quickly faded with the realization that life at home would be almost as scary and challenging as the hospital stay. At first I was afraid to take my eyes off him and certainly afraid to leave his side. His breathing and vital signs needed constant monitoring. His tiny body required regular positioning to prevent skin sores because he wasn't moving enough on his own. Fluid intakes of the special prescription formula had to be recorded. All of those meticulous records provided Christopher's doctors with necessary information between physician's appointments.

Meal times were most challenging. The pediatrician stressed the importance of frequent, small meals, so almost every hour included an attempt to feed my baby. The hospital sent home tiny bottles with special nipples for premature babies, but Christopher often refused to eat. He cried as if he were hungry, and cried when the bottle touched his lips.

Daylight hours felt stressful, but nights seemed even longer. Christopher slept some, but also cried a lot through the night. I rocked and walked and sang and talked, but sometimes he could not be calmed. Despite my attempts to nap when he slept, neither of us had enough rest.

Family and friends tried to help, bringing food and running errands. Sometimes the braver ones volunteered to watch the baby while I slept a little. At least most of his care – changing him, watching him, rocking him – was similar to any newborn's, so those tasks could be done by those who graciously offered. When visitors left, I spent most of my time holding Christopher, trying to comfort him and coaxing him to eat so he wouldn't lose more weight. Sometimes he paused from crying when he heard my singing. Often I only hummed his lullabies, too tired to make any other sounds. We'd sleep in brief spurts, sitting up in a rocking chair with my arms around him, before he'd begin to cry again.

About three months after Christopher came home, a friend of mine brought over her six-month-old infant who'd had a similar due date to Christopher's. She spread out a quilt on the den floor, and placed her daughter there. Her baby rolled over, smiled, cooed, and laughed. Her baby even sat up to hold her own bottle as she eagerly drank. For the first time, I understood the severity of Christopher's delays more clearly. When she left, I hugged Christopher and said aloud to myself, "Stay strong."

At nine-months-old, Christopher still could not roll over without assistance. An hourly timer reminded me to change his position so he would not develop sores on his delicate skin. He could not sit up without the support of a special chair to hold his body upright. The pediatrician didn't expect him to be able to learn to crawl.

I rejoiced at the glimpse of what may have been an occasional smile, but couldn't properly celebrate. I was too worried about his failure to eat. His pediatrician worried with me and referred me to a new specialist who determined Christopher's lack of muscular strength affected his ability to swallow and to suckle. His crying partially stemmed from symptoms of severe reflux, and he couldn't take enough formula to gain weight or receive enough nourishment.

My baby needed a gastrostomy tube.

Surgery went well, but both of us suffered through the post-surgery care. For weeks after the tube's placement into Christopher's stomach, the raw wound circling the tube had to be treated with silver nitrate. The surgeon instructed me to touch the silver nitrate stick to the skin around the tube to facilitate healing. Each time that stick touched my baby's skin, he would scream. I understood the reason for the gastrostomy tube and felt thankful for the nourishment it provided. But I hated that tube from the beginning. Christopher would scream. I would weep.

After the surgical wounds finally healed, the feeding process itself was not difficult at all. Place Christopher into his support chair. Remove the lid from the special formula kept at room temperature. Screw the empty 60cc syringe onto the feeding tube's attachment and slowly add the designated amount prescribed by the doctor to the syringe. Pour in the formula, holding the syringe in the air above the hole in Christopher's stomach. Gravity did all the rest.

The feeding process was trial and error, as were many facets of Christopher's daily care. He suffered when medical professionals misjudged what he needed, and when I didn't know enough to correct them or made mistakes myself. With the gastrostomy feedings, the syringe easily could be held too high, gravity sending an entire serving of formula into my boy's stomach too quickly. Then Christopher suffered reflux, spitting up or vomiting the meal, and crying in discomfort. After a kind nurse's suggestions and with practice, I learned to hold the syringe closer to his body so the formula emptied at a slower rate.

After beginning the feedings via gastrostomy tube, Christopher no longer looked gaunt and undernourished. In fact, too quickly, the opposite problem occurred. While he looked emaciated in his first Christmas photo with the mall's Santa, he appeared overweight in a spring photograph with the same mall's Easter Bunny. Soon I was shopping for a toddler boy's clothes in the six-year racks, and then having to cut off the pants at the knees to hem them. Christopher's obesity began to impact his breathing, and his extra weight made it difficult for me to carry him and move him from his bed to his wheelchair.

Too much time passed before a nutritionist said now he needed to diet! The tube was a blessing, and it was a curse. I vowed to do everything in my power to get Christopher to eat enough by mouth so he wouldn't need a feeding tube.

His doctors also continued to have more questions than answers when it came to his seizures. Christopher began taking seizure medications in the Neonatal Intensive Care Unit right after birth. A pediatric neurologist continued to follow his care, trying different drugs at different doses. Some of Christopher's seizures were barely noticeable except to me. With those, his eyes would move back and forth quickly and he wouldn't respond to me or other stimuli. At other times, his body would suddenly jerk with his face contorted and both of his arms lifted straight out in front of him.

My hourly notes scribbled on college-ruled paper in a three-ring binder traveled with us to every neurologist's appointment. Based on those records, the doctor switched Christopher's doses and medicines often, once even prescribing a new drug requiring daily injections by needle. Nothing seemed to make much difference in whether or not he had seizures, but I began to notice changes related to the medication's timing. Between doses, he showed much more interest in his surroundings; after I gave him the syringes of seizure medicine, he looked lethargic and often slept through the next few hours. A second opinion by a different neurologist confirmed Christopher was vastly overmedicated. Once he came off some of the medicine, he began to smile and to respond to some verbal cues much more regularly.

More and more of my days with Christopher were spent in physicians' offices, in treatments, or in researching a growing list of health concerns. For the first two years, his life and mine revolved around the medical world. As time passed and he missed developmental markers, we saw additional specialists for tests and assessments. I made calls, ordered books and brochures, visited area support groups to try to find information about Christopher's needs and how to help him. His combination of disabilities, especially his lack of language, made it difficult for the medical professionals to assess what he needed.

As the test results from Christopher's appointments came back, I began to learn a new language of vocabulary previously foreign to me – medical conditions' names like microcephaly, support groups' acronyms such as ARC, and a long list of medicines I couldn't pronounce. Test after test brought bad news about Christopher's prognosis.

By his second birthday, Christopher's medical binder bulged with reports from professionals that included pediatric gastroenterologists, neurologists, physical therapists, occupational therapists, early childhood development experts, speech therapists, ophthalmologists, psychologists, and surgeons. They spoke, some gently and others matter-of-factly, of their findings.

"Your son has severe cerebral palsy."

"Christopher is profoundly mentally retarded."

"Your child has microcephaly."

"Christopher's seizures remain uncontrolled."

When those strangers told me Christopher's diagnoses, I usually thanked them and left calmly.

Only one test result left me distraught. One afternoon two weeks after Christopher had an electro-encephalogram to determine brain function, the postal carrier placed a long white envelope in my box, along with an electric bill. Tearing away the end of the envelope while walking back from the mailbox, I saw words something like, "We regret to inform you of your son's inability to see." I remember walking through the house for hours, repeating over and over, "My little boy can't see me. My little boy will never see his mommy. He can't see me."

All those new medical labels didn't mean much on paper, but their reality to Christopher and to me grew more significant. At his two-year-old pediatric checkup, he couldn't sit by himself unless supported in a special seat or wheelchair. He couldn't roll over or crawl or stand. He never was expected to walk or talk. He could not, and probably never would, feed himself or be toilet trained or care for himself in any way.

Each time Christopher visited yet another doctor or specialist, they provided a form requesting information about all of his diagnoses, test results, medications, and treatments. Soon I became weary of the labels and began to describe my son in terms that better gave the picture of who he was to me.

"Tell me about Christopher," a new person at a new medical office would say. I would start by telling them he had the longest eyelashes of anyone they'd ever seen. I'd share how he could cry – and loudly – when he felt hunger or pain. How he'd learned to eat a little bit of pureed food by mouth. How he calmed during my off-key lullabies. "He lights up my entire day with his smile," I'd add.

After two years of constant round-the-clock care, I began to admit to myself that Christopher needed more than I could give him without help. His physical health was fragile after a bout with pneumonia. He needed physical and occupational therapy several times weekly, in addition to the exercises at home. I began to search for agencies that would provide me with more training, and discovered a service that offered respite care when I needed to run an errand or even just take a nap.

One afternoon I answered my phone to hear a stranger's voice offering me more help than expected – and help I wasn't sure I wanted. She introduced herself as the director of a local residential center for children with developmental disabilities, and briefly described the services provided to each child served. She said my son's pediatrician had suggested she call. "Would you be interested in meeting to talk about a placement for Christopher?" she asked.

With my trembling hand holding the receiver, I almost slammed down the phone, but instead took a deep breath and listened. She invited me to tour the facility the next week. In parting words, she gently added that the opening would be filled quickly. After the call ended, I couldn't eat or sleep for two days. Why would I even visit such a place? How could I ever want my child to live somewhere other than at home? After a few days of researching, telephoning Christopher's doctors, pacing and praying, thinking and crying, I called her for an appointment.

Surprisingly at my visit, the residential home seemed like, well, a home! The facility allowed only ten children at a time as residents, so the building's size and design felt welcoming. The layout included the children's bedrooms and bathrooms, several large communal living spaces, a kitchen, and a dining area. All the spaces felt homey and happy.

The professionals on staff held impressive credentials and experience. Regular staff included round-the-clock registered nurses, nursing care technicians, a dietician and cook, physical therapists, occupational therapists, and an on-call doctor. Christopher's pediatrician even served as their primary pediatric consultant. The director shared a copy of the center's policies, a parent's handbook, and a history of the nonprofit's development.

From the tour and additional research, I began to realize what this residential placement might mean for Christopher. He'd be monitored by medical staff 24 hours a day and seven days a week. Professionals would design and implement ongoing plans for his specific nutritional needs, medications, and therapy treatments. Physical and occupational therapists would assess and treat him onsite twice weekly, while staff would perform his necessary exercises for range of motion on a daily basis.

And, miraculously, this amazing facility was only 20 minutes from my home so I could visit at any time. He could come home, even for overnight stays. I'd be just as involved in his overall care, but a part of his team to plan and implement everything he needed. And I could be his Mommy first and foremost instead of his nurse and therapist. I could sleep more than minutes at a time, and also could work. I was under no obligation for him to live there forever.

The children's center had one opening, and they'd offered it to Christopher. Even after finally admitting this opportunity was best, the decision still was excruciatingly difficult. Finally, I called the director to accept the placement. I thanked her, hung up the phone, and spent the rest of the day rocking my son.

Despite all of the reasons why this decision was the best for us both, I still struggled when he began spending much of his time there. Visiting daily – and sometimes more than once a day – helped. At my visits, I brought new books to read and sometimes gifts of toys and clothes. We sat together on the couch in the living room rocking and singing our favorite songs. I still took him to all of his appointments and attended every team meeting with the medical professionals. I quickly grew to love all of the staff and the other children who resided there.

Soon the positive changes in Christopher's demeanor and health were obvious to me. He seemed much more alert, responding to the presence of the other children. Every staff member treated him as if they genuinely loved him and all the children. As the nursing staff and doctor closely monitored his diet and medications, he attained a healthier weight and became less lethargic. Staff reported he had begun to take more bites of pureed food by mouth, so his tube feeding amounts could be decreased a little. He grew more attentive to people's actions around him, turning his head in the direction of conversations and noise. My boy seemed happy.

Although he probably had the most severe cognitive disabilities of any child residing there, Christopher began to show progress. Always I believed Christopher understood much more than he could communicate back to us. As his care team began to work daily with Christopher, they began to believe that too.

One extraordinary day his physical therapist showed me how she'd give the verbal cue, "Christopher, move your leg." Never before had he responded to that cue, but on that day, his leg would move slightly every time she said those words. The therapist beamed as she reported that success to the team in our next meeting. We all felt so proud, knowing his great effort surpassed an athlete's successful marathon.

With his weight down, his medications more balanced, and his body accustomed to daily physical therapy, Christopher improved his responses to others, especially to children. With his roommates' noisy, sometimes rowdy, verbal sounds and movement in wheelchairs, he paid attention. He smiled more often and sometimes vocalized a sound of laughter.

In addition to my daily visits, Christopher had lots of other visitors. Families were always welcome to visit at any time of the night or day, and many events provided a time for extended family members to gather. My parents and siblings joined the center's celebration for Halloween when he dressed like the Lone Ranger in his cowboy hat and boots, and again for a Christmas party where he smiled during the carol singing. Family, friends, and staff joined to celebrate his birthdays, featuring Snoopy and three candles as he turned three, and a fire truck lined with four candles the next year. We sang "Happy Birthday, dear Christopher," and he laughed.

I had no doubts that I'd made the right decision for my son's well-being. Yet, despite knowing Christopher needed all the facility offered him, I never stopped missing him at home. I worked extra hours to stay busy and visited him for as long as possible each day. Each time I started wondering if I could manage his care back at home, he would suffer a setback in his eating or sleeping or general health.

Christopher's critical need for advanced medical care proved itself several months later during another bout with a respiratory infection that turned into pneumonia. The facility's nurse quickly diagnosed the situation and transported him to the appropriate hospital where he spent several weeks. I stayed at the hospital, sleeping on the couch in a waiting room. Throughout his long hospitalization – almost two months, I went home only one night.

During that stay, Christopher suffered cardiac arrest and nearly died. When a nurse summoned me to intensive care, the attending doctor told me Christopher's heart had stopped and then started back on its own. The physician then said to me, "For your sake, I did not know whether to hope he lived or died." I didn't trust my voice to say the words I wanted. I knew I'd refuse for that doctor to see us again. My angry conversation with him would wait. Instead, I stepped past the physician and into the unit to see my little boy.

Beside Christopher's bed, I took his hand in mine and leaned over to kiss his forehead. Then I whispered, "I'm so proud of you, Chrissy. You were brave and strong."

Chapter 4: Eating Chocolate and Dirt

During Christopher's hospital stay for yet another bout with pneumonia, I walked down to the hospital gift shop to look for something he might like, and returned to his bedside with a gift box holding a plush white unicorn with a gold horn. "Mommy brought a surprise," I whispered, placing the plush under his hand when he stirred from napping. He felt the soft material and flashed a flicker of a smile.

With a winding of the toy's key, the unicorn began to play my favorite song, "Somewhere Over the Rainbow." I sang along to the tinkling accompaniment. Christopher grinned. Later, on my way to the hospital cafeteria, I went back to buy a second unicorn just like the first – one to stay in his bed at the children's center and one for his bed at home when he came to sleep over on weekends or holidays.

Christopher loved music, so often his gifts on special occasions were music boxes and toys that made sounds. The unicorn became a favorite of his and mine. On nighttime visits to the center, I'd stay late enough to tuck him into his little bed in the room he shared with two other boys. After the staff bathed him and dressed him in soft pajamas, they'd lift him into his bed. We'd read a story and, after goodnight kisses, we'd listen to his unicorn's song play again and again, winding down to silence. Then I'd tell him I loved him and walk quickly out of the building alone, making certain I could reach my car before crying. Yes, Dorothy, "There's no place like home," and I wanted my little boy at home with me.

The care team's quarterly meetings began to focus on Christopher's homecoming. Despite his progress at the center, I'd never stopped wanting him back home and preparing for that day. The leadership and staff supported my decision. Together, we began to make the plans for his transition to home care. Some of the professionals who worked with the facility's children were contracted employees, so they could treat Christopher at either location. His physical therapy equipment could be kept at home. With respite services, an on-call nurse, and part-time help, Christopher finally could be home and yet have all the services needed for his development.

Only one hold-up delayed our plans: Christopher's baby sister. Arrangements were in place to bring him home several months before her birth, but then she tried to come into the world much too early – at only four months into my pregnancy. My obstetrician ordered complete bed rest until her due date. Long days, weeks, and months passed slowly waiting impatiently for my daughter's birth and my son's return home.

During the best part of those months, I created a bond with my little girl before her birth. I read books, sang silly songs, spoke French, and recited the multiplication tables to her. I talked constantly to my baby, telling her about her big brother. Those peaceful times helped a little in calming my anxiety about her birth. I had been afraid to be pregnant again because of Christopher's birth issues, and now my daughter was at-risk in utero.

Besides concerns for the new baby's health, the absence from my son was the worst part of those months. The obstetrician insisted on my quiet confinement at home, ruling out not only Christopher's homecoming, but also my daily visits to the center. The staff there helped me stay as connected as possible. They telephoned each day, placing Christopher's wheelchair beside the speaker of their office phone and reporting to me how he'd respond to my voice and words. The staff, family, and friends brought him home to me for short visits, while family members visited him at the center in my place.

The day my obstetrician stopped the medication preventing preterm labor, contractions began. Soon after midnight, a doctor delivered my beautiful baby girl via C-section under an epidural. The moment the nurse handed her to me, I wept with gratitude because my baby girl safely arrived and because now Christopher could come home again.

Home now was Jack's favorite place, and he preferred not to leave the property. He'd settled into the household routine and seemed much calmer except during trips to the vet's. Jack knew how to run quickly outside, despite any scary noises, for bathroom time and often stayed outside long enough to play with the other pups. He loved to run after a tennis ball – at least for a few moments until he tried to eat it. He continued to amaze everyone who met him with his athleticism.

I bought Jack lots of toys but he decimated them in record time, destroying the exterior of any plush, ball, or chew toy. His ability to extract a squeaker from inside a dog toy marked "indestructible" became a family joke. I'd set the timer and laugh as he ran to the toy, grabbed it, carried it to the far side of the room, and promptly chewed it into bits before I removed all the pieces so he wouldn't swallow any part. Strangely, he still never harmed his banana toy. He always mouthed it with gentleness. He snuggled beside it in his bed each night.

One morning while brushing his coat to remove the grass and leaves from playtime, I noticed a growth on Jack's left back leg. We'd just been to the vet's office for a checkup two weeks earlier and the leg looked fine then. At a walk-in appointment that afternoon, the vet examined Jack's leg and said the growth probably was a benign cyst, but should be removed. Other dogs in my care, including Ozzie and several foster pups, had needed cysts removed before, but always those lumps were benign. The surgery went well and Jack's recovery was easy enough, but the pathology report came back as "malignant." Still, the surgeon believed he'd gotten all the cancer.

Maybe I would have worried longer, but my thoughts were on Patches' health. Patches' heart murmur was discovered as a young dog, but had not affected his health until his 10th birthday. In his early teens, his breathing patterns changed noticeably, his at-rest breathing always too fast. A trip to the vet and then to a specialist confirmed that Patches had congestive heart failure. Medicines and lifestyle changes helped ease his symptoms, but gradually his coughing and breathing grew worse.

Finally the day came when Patches needed to make his last trip to the specialty vet's office. As I gathered his blanket and favorite treats, Ozzie and Jack seemed to know they were saying goodbye to their old friend. Patches even gave Jack – who still always followed him around as if he were a hero to Jack – a wag. When the car returned without dear Patches, the other pups were quiet and solemn for a few days. Jack seemed especially sad.

To try to cheer Jack, I scheduled another Blessing of the Animals at the same rescue where Jack's adoption occurred, and decided to take Jack with me. Staff there loved him and we'd kept in touch, but now enough time had passed that he'd be okay to visit. Previously I felt concerned if we visited, he would think I was returning him.

Imagine my surprise, along with a little dismay, when I opened his car door to put on his leash, and he jumped out of the vehicle and ran straight to the front door. A volunteer saw him coming and opened the door. He ran back to the little room where he'd spent his recovery. The staff and I laughed, and I loved seeing him greeting all of his former friends there, but I stayed a little worried that he would not want to leave.

However, when it was time to go, he eagerly let me put on his leash and ran right out the door to the car without looking back. Good to visit, and good to go home!

The sight of Christopher's smile on his Homecoming Day from the children's center was a scene I always will cherish. Long before the day and time determined best by staff, we all had worked out careful details about his home care, held a "Good-bye" party for staff and our family, and moved all of his equipment and belongings home.

On that morning's drive to the center, I sang at the top of my lungs and felt as if I floated from the car through the parking lot. The director stood waiting for me at the front door. She coyly smiled and said she wasn't sure of Christopher's location. Playing along with her, we pretended an elaborate hide-and-seek adventure in front of delighted staff. I walked first to his bedroom, and then to the kitchen and dining area. No Christopher to be found. Finally I tried the director's office only to spot him, blue wheelchair adorned with celebratory ribbons. Christopher's smile – that's too ordinary a word – radiated joy with a sparkle in his eyes, cheeks rosy, lips spread ear to ear. I've never seen a bigger, more beautiful smile.

Without a doubt, he knew he was going home!

Jack and Ozzie settled into their routine of friendship and fun. They dashed around the yard together, and rested side by side on a blanket in the living room. When an early snow fell, the pups delighted in chasing one another through the white yard, and tentatively biting the mounds of snow. For Christmas, Ms. Santa brought them special treats and new collars, along with a squeaky toy for Ozzie and tennis balls for Jack.

Jack now seemed confident in the household and he began to vocalize his happiness. He still loved to eat and began barking at me during meal preparation times as if to say "Hurry! Feed me! I'm hungry!" If he became excited about company or playing or just because Ozzie was enthusiastic, Jack first would bark loudly. If the excitement grew, he would put his nose into the air and begin to howl.

Occasionally – thankfully it didn't happen often – he would dream in the middle of the night and start howling. On those times, I'd be sleeping soundly and then suddenly sit straight up in the bed, startled by the sound of my beagle's howl.

One of Jack's favorite days was laundry day. As soon as a clean comforter covered my bed, he'd run and hop as fast as he could up the steps to the bed so he could wallow all over the bedding. He seemed to grin from floppy ear to ear as he'd lean one side of his head down to the bedding and run around in circles, wagging with glee. A freshly-washed quilt in his bed brought the same reaction. Sometimes I'd add an extra laundry day to my week just to watch him.

He grew stronger and faster. Jack became the most athletic dog I knew. With so much of his weight on the front of his body, his front paw spread wider. Muscles bulged in his legs. He dashed around the yard, playing with Ozzie. He chased the tennis balls faster than ever. He jumped over small plants in the yard.

At my rest times, he would climb up the steps with Ozzie instead of climbing into his own bed on the floor. He'd wallow on the bedding for a few moments, but quickly settle into his nap position beside me. I loved to watch him dreaming. He always seemed to dream happy dreams. At least I hoped that was the case.

When he'd sleep soundly and dream, his heavy tail would begin to thump. Then his paws twitched. Soon he'd move all his legs a little. His shoulder muscle at the top of the missing leg would move too. I believed he had all four legs in his dreams. Whether in his dreams or in the daylight's reality, he never seemed to miss his leg.

The household became busier, louder, and happier with both Christopher and his new sister settled at home. His physical and occupational therapists now came to our house. Christopher stayed more alert with his lowered dose of seizure medicines, and he smiled more with Jessica's presence. On her baptism day, he fussed about wearing his new pin-striped blue and white suit but sat quietly for their photos together. Both children enjoyed our reading, music, and dancing times that involved range-of-motion stretches for Christopher and the Twist or Hokey Pokey for Jessica.

All of the holidays meant special decorations, foods, and activities. Halloween may have been different than at my neighbors' homes, but our celebration brought the traditional fun of carving a pumpkin and dressing in costumes. Christopher's wheelchair couldn't easily be rolled through the neighborhood, so friends and family came to our house instead, bringing small toys and food instead of candy. Christopher dressed in a pumpkin costume sewn by a friend. In every photo, he stuck out his lower lip. He was not a happy jack-o-lantern!

With Jessica present during mealtimes, Christopher began to be more tolerant of staying at the table long enough to try new foods. All of his dishes had to be pureed into the consistency of baby food, and usually he spat out more than he'd accept – until the day they both discovered chocolate pudding. She squealed with glee at her first bite. He seemed to understand her delight because he opened widely to taste the pudding. He swallowed the entire bite and began smacking for more.

He consumed only one other food with more enthusiasm than chocolate. A friend helped me take the children to the county fair, where we pushed Jessica's stroller and Christopher's wheelchair side by side. We managed to take them on the merry-go-round, my neighbor holding Christopher in the saddle of one steed, while I clutched Jess on the horse in front. We visited the livestock barn where both children wrinkled their noses at the smell of manure from the cows, horses, and hogs there.

By far though, Christopher's favorite part of the fair was his first taste of cotton candy. As I put the stuff to his lips, he took it hesitantly. Then, as the syrupy sweet began to dissolve in his mouth, he opened his eyes widely, smacked loudly, and grinned in silly delight.

In early November, the children's choir director at church heard me mention how Christopher loved music. "Would you like to bring him to choir rehearsals?" he offered. I didn't hesitate to accept the invitation, and Christopher didn't miss a rehearsal. He sat attentively while the other children sang, laughed, and danced around him.

When the children gave their Christmas concert, Christopher's wheelchair was placed in the middle of the front row. When the children began to sing, he began to make noises – something he'd never done in rehearsals. His moaning soon began to be louder than some of the voices, and I grew concerned others might be upset. Instead, the audience stood and cheered with their applause when the concert ended. As I began to roll Christopher down the altar area's ramp, I felt a tug on my skirt hem and looked down to see a little girl, one of the choir's members. "Thank you for letting Christopher sing with us," she said with a smile.

During Jack's adventures outside, he still had to be monitored closely to be certain he didn't eat anything strange, including dirt. If he began digging with his front paw and trying to eat dirt, he would not stop until I went out with his leash and brought him back inside. He definitely possessed the stubbornness trait prevalent in beagles.

At some point his odd eating behaviors moved from the yard to inside the house. I'd leave home to run an errand, and be surprised to find one book off of my bookcase with a small corner of a page missing. I was unsure why he began consuming paper inside, but the behavior worsened. He chewed the corner off of my new Julia Child's cookbook. He even ate the middle out of a book I'd mistakenly left on the end table – a newly purchased dog training guide!

One day Ozzie tried to top Jack's mischievous eating habits. I came home from the grocery store to find a bag of chocolates on the floor. I have no idea how Jack knocked off the bag from the far edge of the table, but one piece had fallen out at Ozzie's feet. He'd chewed through the wrapper and managed to lick out most of the chocolate. I grabbed the wrapper and the open bag off the floor, worried that Ozzie had consumed enough to make him ill. Thankfully, he showed no signs of sickness but afterward, every single time I'd eat chocolate, Ozzie would beg for it.

The worst incident for Jack's strange eating habits occurred as I taught a class for the local college. In the middle of grading student papers, I had to leave for an appointment. When I returned home, Jack had eaten bites out of my students' homework assignments. I attempted to piece together bits of paper across my kitchen table, but my efforts were futile because Jack had consumed some of the pieces. I couldn't give only part of my class their grades, and I wouldn't ask students to redo their assignments.

My students loved my opening announcement for the next day's class: "<u>My</u> dog ate <u>your</u> homework!" I gave them all A's.

Chapter 5: Dragons on the Beach

Five candles on a chocolate ice-cream cake. Shiny bows atop boxes wrapped in bright primary colors. A chorus of "Happy Birthday to you!" sung enthusiastically, if a little off-key, by family who adored him. Christopher's fifth birthday party possessed all the usual elements for a child's celebration, except one: Christopher had no friends there.

Other children had play dates to romp on a playground's swings or race down the slide. Christopher spent his afternoons in physical therapy with his arms and legs being moved by the therapist. Friends' youngsters caught measles from their playmates, while Christopher couldn't go into the pediatrician's office for a checkup without having a parent move their child away from him to the other side of the room. Moms in the mall complained about having to buy yet another birthday gift for their child to take to a weekend party. My son had no invitations.

He definitely responded with attentiveness and sometimes a smile when my friends occasionally brought their children as they dropped by to share a homemade casserole or pie. He smiled and sometimes laughed during the Children's Choir practice at church. At the children's facility, he'd had the constant company of other children. He loved any time his baby sister was nearby, but she still was too young to play. Yes, Christopher needed friends.

I decided to find a local preschool where he could interact with other children for several hours once or twice weekly. His medical team offered suggestions for his participation, including sending a nurse who would be right at his side throughout the few hours in attendance. I planned to pay for a full slot at the preschool so Christopher's attendance would not be a hardship on the preschool. His pediatrician and support team prepared recommendations.

With preparations finalized, I couldn't wait to enroll Christopher as soon as possible. The largest church in town reportedly had a good daycare and preschool program. I telephoned the church and asked if there were openings. "Yes!" the program's director enthusiastically answered. She invited me to visit later that week.

Documents and photographs in a folder, I arrived 20 minutes earlier than our appointment. The director greeted me, showed me around the daycare, and then began to ask about my child. I first told her Christopher's age and showed her a head shot photograph. "So handsome! What amazing eyelashes!" she said.

Next I shared aspects of his personality and his life.

"Christopher loves music and is in our children's choir at church."

"His favorite activities at home are listening to me reading funny books, playing beside his sister, and eating anything chocolate."

"He doesn't like waiting in lines for the movies or doctor's appointments, and he hates any dish with tomatoes."

Then, after taking a deep breath, I told the director about his special needs, assuring her those would not impact his presence at the program. I told her I'd pay for a full slot in their program, but initially wanted to bring him only one day weekly for two hours. The local pediatrician's letter of recommendation, and those of others who worked with Christopher, were in the documents provided. I showed her the credentials of the registered nurse who'd be on site in case they had questions or concerns (and who could stay outside the facility or right beside Christopher, as they wished). I explained how Christopher's gastrostomy tube fit inside his shirts, out of the way, between feedings, and how he would not need feedings during preschool.

Finally I showed her photos of Christopher in his cool blue wheelchair and his support chair. He looked handsome and happy.

Her smiling face never changed.

Yet when I called back the next day to say I'd completed the form she'd given me at the beginning of the tour, she said there had been a mistake and there were no openings. I asked her how they could have had three openings in his class the day before, and have none the next morning. She said only, "There's no place for him here."

I didn't give up. The next week I visited the largest church preschool in the next town over, just 15 minutes away. They too had openings, they said. I went through my pitch again. At least they were more honest. The director immediately said they would not allow Christopher to attend. "The children will be afraid of him," she insisted.

One morning I watched Jack devour his breakfast with his usual beagle gusto, but noticed Ozzie ate only a few bites and didn't seem to feel well. By midday, Ozzie wanted to go outside several times an hour. At the vet's office the next morning, the tests confirmed Ozzie was experiencing kidney failure. The good news: a special prescription food and medication could help the symptoms for an indefinite period of time. The bad news: eventually the symptoms would worsen. After his treatments began, Ozzie seemed much better. Still, I worried and couldn't bear to think about the day that might come without my little furry soul mate.

Only a month after Ozzie's diagnosis, I discovered the new mass on Jack's leg. At nap time with a new comforter on my bed, Jack climbed the steps and began to wallow in glee. As he rolled around and over, I saw the bulge on the same leg where he'd previously had surgery. Turning on the nightstand's light to see more clearly, I ran my fingers over the raised place and said aloud a word I hadn't thought in almost two years: "Cancer."

The vet took one look at Jack's leg the next day, and scheduled surgery as quickly as possible. The procedure was long and difficult because the tumor had grown around a major vessel in his leg. Although the skilled surgeon tried to remove as much tissue around the tumor as possible, the post-surgery pathology report confirmed that cancerous cells remained. The vet believed the cancer would soon return.

Jack's veterinary office referred me to an oncology expert at the same specialized veterinary practice where Patches had received treatment. At the first appointment, the oncologist advised radiation as the only choice for treatment in Jack's case. Typically for this cancer, the dog's leg would be removed. In Jack's case, he already lost one leg and could not lose another.

The radiation oncologist spoke positively about radiation treatments. I looked at the research numbers and knew the odds were not as good as his presentation. Yet no other choice existed for Jack's treatment. The aggressive cancer likely would return quickly unless he received radiation. The treatment would be expensive, but the family emergency fund would cover some of it and a loan from the home equity line would take care of the rest.

The most difficult part of the decision was the consideration for Jack's potential side effects and the logistics of daily treatments that lasted for weeks. The facility gave me options to leave Jack with them throughout the week and come back for him to be at home on weekends, or even to keep him for the entire treatment schedule. I knew Jack would be afraid whatever the choice, but I was not going to let him face this alone. The routine would be grueling for me too. The drive to the center would take about an hour, sometimes more, with the heavy traffic in that urban area. I arranged for transportation help on some days, and vowed to drive Jack there myself on the others.

I spoke with my pups' vet before making the final decision. He kindly gave me permission to take either road, saying that dogs did not think about the length of time on earth or what they may have missed. He told me he knew my decision would be made out of love. When I thought about Jack's struggles in his early life, I decided he deserved as much lifetime with love and joy as I could give him. Radiation, it would be.

On the first morning for treatment, Jack wagged as we headed to the car, and eagerly hopped into his usual spot on the passenger side of my two-seater car. After an initial anxious 15 minutes, he slowed his panting, lulled by the car system's gentle music and the car's movement. Soon he drifted to a light sleep. That first drive and treatment went smoothly, and he happily jumped back into the car for the return trip. His travel bag held special treats for an after-radiation reward, along with fresh water. On the way home, I sang to him when traffic was lighter.

For the first two weeks of his treatments, he'd jump out of the car at the medical center and come inside without hesitation. After each day's registration, the friendly technician soon called his name and led him back to the treatment room. Each radiation treatment required anesthesia and recovery time.

Too soon Jack began experiencing painful side effects of the radiation, and finally a horrible open wound that obviously caused him agony. Still, he faithfully would go out with me and get into the car at home. Yet he refused to get out of the car when we arrived at the clinic, so a staff member would come out and lift him from the car. He hesitated to go into the building, but still always followed the staff person down the hallway to the treatment area.

I'd watch him hop down that hallway, his hound ears flopping, until he disappeared around the corner. Then my eyes would fill with tears and I'd try not to cry before reaching the car.

I spent his hours of treatment time in different ways: eating breakfast at a local restaurant a mile down the road, reading and writing in the parking lot, walking around a nearby park. A few times I tried to stay in the nice waiting area, but my heart soon felt too heavy because of so many other dogs and cats who came into the place. They too had serious illnesses. Many were there for radiation. Some of their humans were there to get opinions and came out crying, their pets close beside them. Some people entered the building with their furry companions and left without them, tears flowing.

By the final day of radiation, Jack and I both dreaded going. The people there were wonderful, but the radiation had excruciating side effects for Jack. On the way home from his last treatment, I kept apologizing to Jack, telling him how brave and strong he was. And I told him he'd never have to go through anything else so painful and scary. No matter what.

In our follow-up appointments for the next year, the doctors repeatedly voiced their belief the cancer was gone. I celebrated that news and hoped they were right.

I didn't give up on my dream for Christopher to attend a preschool. After two more programs declined his enrollment, I visited a preschool center in a smaller church nearby. The director never hesitated. She quickly said they'd be blessed for Christopher to come and knew the children would learn greatly from his presence in their class. Overcome with gratitude and relief, I remember hugging her and wanting to dance my way to the car.

When his first day of preschool came, Christopher smiled all the way from home to the church. As he rolled through the school's door in his wheelchair, the children in his class ran to meet him. Not afraid at all, of course. He loved every day spent there, and the teachers and children adored him.

By the time the holiday season arrived, I found handmade Christmas cards from his preschool friends sent home in Christopher's lunch box. Ms. Santa shopped for a Snoopy music box for Christopher, a block set and puzzles for Jessica, books and clothes for them both. For a new Christmas tradition, the children donned festive matching brother-sister clothes for a photographer's session. Both brother and sister wore a Rudolph reindeer top, complete with a tasseled red nose.

On Christmas Day Ms. Claus brought special treats for Jack and Ozzie, along with new collars. They also each received a toy, a plush squeaky dragon in a bright green color. Ozzie loved soft, small toys. In the past, he would gently nibble on plush animals' ears or limbs, but never hard enough to break through the material. Jack, on the other hand, always quickly tore off limbs and ears, chewed out the squeakers, all while I raced to remove the toy so he wouldn't swallow it and begin squeaking himself!

On that Christmas morning, Ozzie eagerly took his dragon toy and began nursing it, as expected. I carefully watched Jack, expecting him to destroy the dragon as he did every toy except for his beloved banana. Surprisingly, he took it into his mouth gently and carried it around but never gnawed on it. He treated it just as tenderly over the next few weeks, so the dragon toy joined with his banana as part of our bedtime ritual. Jack nuzzled and slept with both toys under his head or front paw. Like his first-ever toy, the yellow banana, Jack seemed to treasure that dragon.

Despite the loving acceptance of family and close friends, strangers began to react more negatively to Christopher when we went out to public places. At one pediatrician's office for a regular checkup, I rolled Christopher's wheelchair into the "well" section of the waiting rooms. We waited an hour, so Christopher needed a little formula through his tube. A few moments after the quick feeding, two different parents moved their children to a space in the "sick" room away from us.

When Christopher's wheelchair traveled through the mall's corridor as we shopped for his clothes, some people crossed to the other side of the aisle. Others approached us and asked the strangest things. "What's wrong with him?" "Why is he jerking like that?" A few even questioned me about the cause for his disabilities. "Did you fall during pregnancy?" "Drink?" "Smoke?"

Even with those who knew us, I found it increasingly difficult to talk to people about Christopher. Some of the most well-meant comments frustrated me the most. I began to respond in my head, keeping silent with my mouth.

"The Creator only gives disabled children to special parents." *So my child's suffering is a reward to me? To him?*

"I'm praying for a miracle cure to make him normal." *Could the Holy One not fix this without that prayer? And what's normal?*

"We're never given more than we can handle." *Wrong. Just wrong.*

"It's God's will." *Really? So an all-powerful Creator who is pure and perfect Love willed an innocent child to suffer?*

As Ozzie's kidney condition worsened, Jack and Ozzie's interactions began to change. Jack would go down the outside steps and wait for Ozzie to come play, but Ozzie ignored Jack's invitation. At Ozzie's next check, his tests showed his kidney function was decreasing. Soon he needed trips to the vet's office for them to empty his bladder – initially twice weekly, but then every other day. At first he responded well to treatments and tests showed good results.

Two months later, the vet solemnly reported the news that his blood creatinine and urea nitrogen levels had skyrocketed. My heart sank because those numbers meant the every-day treatments were no longer working. The technician gave extra fluids and made my dear pup another appointment for two days later.

That evening Ozzie began to tremble, first slightly and then violently. He ran outside where he vomited until he had nothing left in his stomach. I carried him from the yard, back into the house, and upstairs to my library – the place where I'd moved his bed, where I wanted to spend years longer with him looking out the window while I wrote at my desk.

I placed him gently in his bed and tried to comfort him. Even with covers placed around him, he began to shake all over again. He wasn't cold, I realized. He was in severe pain, and I knew I was the only one who could end that pain.

I wrapped him in a blanket and grabbed a piece of chocolate. I'd decided months before that at his time of death, he could have the chocolate he always wanted. But at the emergency vet's office, they gave him an injection to dull the pain. Although I offered him the chocolate as we awaited the vet to come and help him leave this life, he didn't take it from my hand.

I held him and rocked him and wept until the last breath left his body. Still, I didn't want to leave and stayed there holding him as long as I could until I handed over his little precious body for cremation. My lap dog, my protector, my little Ozzie was gone.

After Ozzie's death, Jack became more fearful again. He didn't want to leave the house, and he especially didn't want me to leave him. If I left the house for more than a brief time, friends stayed with him. He was more terrified than ever of loud noises and especially storms.

Life seemed too difficult in every direction I faced. I often felt too tired to breathe, and yet couldn't sleep even when the house had been quiet for hours. I couldn't seem to write or even to journal. I needed a drastic change. I longed to escape.

Soon open suitcases stood in the living room floor. Piles of laundry went from the washing machine and dryer straight into bags and boxes. Friends delivered used cardboard boxes to hold kitchen dishes and books.

I never hesitated about life's next direction. I headed for the beach.

That first winter at the beach brought the solitude I needed, and my happiest days yet with the children. We celebrated Christopher's sixth birthday there with his favorite chocolate cake. After his party, we marveled at the rare sight of a few snowflakes falling onto the sand.

On another winter day, we carried bread crumbs to the shoreline. One of my favorite photographs of Christopher portrays him in his blue wheelchair, dressed in a coat, a scarf, and a white toboggan with his name in blue trim, while a hundred seagulls circle him on the beach. His sister stands beside him with her hand on his arm. Neither of them was afraid of the sounds of rough sea waves crashing or of squawking birds vying for bread crumbs. On the other hand, I'm not fond of swooping creatures, so I was the photographer and as far away from the action as the camera's scope would allow.

Valentine's Day brought craft and cooking fun. Both children had sticky hands from gluing lacy hearts onto pink and red construction paper, and sticky faces from licking the icing off homemade sugar cookies. We sang love songs and proclaimed "I love you!" in shouts and whispers throughout the holiday.

On a warmer, but windy, March day, we took a kite down beside the ocean. When we had it flying high, I tied it to Christopher's wheelchair and all the passersby watched it soar. Then as the wind shifted and slowed, we watched it fall – right atop one of the next-door buildings.

The children and I dyed Easter eggs and hid them, first inside and then on the beach. The Easter Bunny delivered spring clothes, sand buckets, and a huge silly-looking white rabbit dressed in pastels. At the mall, the children posed beside yet another Easter Bunny before we shopped for new church frocks.

Jessica's second birthday party featured cupcakes, a new doll, and her first attempt at blowing out candles. She tried to coax Christopher to eat the foods I pulverized for him in the blender. He preferred tasting the icing from her party's cake.

In late spring, Clara came into our lives. Early after we moved, I tried using a temporary nursing service for help with Christopher's care, but the faces were different on most days and that didn't work well for continuity of his physical therapy and medical needs. Luckily a new friend told me about a nursing assistant she knew whose long-time client recently died. Clara was seeking a new family with whom to work. At our first meeting, I knew Clara would be perfect for the children because of her compassion, as well as her skills. Quickly she became a beloved part of our family and an invaluable caregiver to Christopher and Jessica.

During summer's hottest months, we made more frequent visits back to see family and friends. We also had lots of visitors who liked spending time with us while seeing the ocean too.

When autumn arrived, I enrolled Christopher in a new preschool class, and he came home with sandbox sand in his tennis shoes and love notes in his lunch box. His new teacher often sent me progress notes and mentioned how much his classmates learned from Christopher's presence.

No matter the season, our evening routine was my favorite part of every day. Clara and I would prepare an early supper, nibbling our own meal as we fed the children. We moved from kitchen to the piano, where I'd play familiar Disney tunes while we sang to Christopher, and laughed at Jessica and Clara dancing. Then Clara would walk with Jessica to the nearby park for swinging and running, while I held Christopher on my lap to rock and talk. I'd always tell him he was the "man of the house," and share news of the week ahead. When Jess and Clara returned, bath time preceded a little television time. Christopher loved to watch Alf and Pee Wee Herman and fussed if he was not in front of the TV for those shows. Jessica liked Smurfs, but Christopher didn't, so he fussed then too.

Jack had never taken a car trip as far as the drive to the beach. He seemed anxious for the first hour, but then settled down for a long nap. (I think he felt better after we'd passed the distance for our usual vet's trip.) When we stopped for a break, he trembled about getting out to potty at a strange place, but settled again when he was back in his bed riding.

His first few days beside the ocean were filled with new and scary experiences. He took his first elevator ride, and nervously met other neighborhood dogs on our early morning walks. He was afraid of the sound of the ocean even from the grassy area meant for dogs to use for their bathroom area, so I tried taking him across the street to a vacant lot. He was afraid of the noise of the cars.

His worst fears as he adjusted to the new surroundings heightened when a tropical system brought severe thunderstorms. I drew the curtains each time the lightning began flashing, and played happy music as loudly as possible without bothering neighbors to try hiding the boom of the thunder. He wasn't fooled. He trembled and tried to run to safe places throughout every storm.

When the weather cleared, he soon began to relax a little. By the end of our first week at the beach, he hesitantly crept toward the sliding glass door overlooking the ocean. Little by little, he stepped toward and finally through the door onto the porch.

I spent hours each day writing and Jack sat beside me on the couch. Sometimes he'd stand beside the picture window and bark a little at dogs walking on the beach.

I love the memory of the day Jack first walked onto the beach. Already we'd prepared by walking together from the grassy area to the top of the ramp that led down to the ocean. On that sunny morning, we walked to the top of the ramp, and then I kept walking. As soon as my feet and his paws touched the sand, he put his beagle nose to the sandy ground – and he was off!

Nose down, he ran straight toward the ocean as fast as he could move, almost dragging me behind him. I couldn't believe he wasn't afraid! And then, about six feet from the water's edge, he suddenly lifted his nose where apparently he was breathing in so many delicious and new smells, and realized he was in front of the huge ocean. He screeched to a halt! And he began dragging me back toward the ramp in the opposite direction. I laughed and stumbled, but we made it back.

At the beach Jack's heart and mine began to heal a little. We snuggled and played during the days. And I tucked him into his bed each night with his banana. But I couldn't seem to find his dragon toy.

I spent as much time as possible with the children down on the beach. On moderate days – not too hot and humid – I'd spread out a beach towel and sit with Christopher on it while Jessica played in the sand. Sometimes she and I would make hoppy toad houses with Christopher's feet. He smiled when she put the cool sand between his toes.

On other pleasant days, we'd roll and walk down the beach. I'd push Christopher's chair on the packed sand and Jessica would run and dance beside us.

On one of our walks, I noticed something different on the beach far away in the distance. Then as we grew closer and closer, I couldn't believe what I was seeing. There before us was a huge dragon created from sand. The creator of the dragon sand sculpture had somehow colored the sand green and the dragon even had fire from its mouth. The size was immense with the dragon's head at least six feet across, and its full body the length of three school buses.

The children and I stayed there beside the dragon as long as we could. As the sun began to set and we started back toward the house, I remember feeling sad because I knew the beautiful dragon wouldn't last through the night's high tide.

Back home at bedtime, I wound up Christopher's music box topped with a dragon and a boy, and sang the words to the tinkling sound, "Puff the magic dragon, lived by the sea." Christopher laughed and I laughed. I sang, "And frolicked in the autumn mist in a land called Honahlee." We laughed again and I repeated that chorus.

I sang only the chorus, never singing the verses to Christopher. I didn't remember the rest of the words.

Chapter 6: Butterfly Kisses and Angel Wings

No matter what the rest of those busy days held, our bedtime rituals remained the same. Faces washed. Teeth brushed. Bedtime stories read aloud and then repeated, usually more than once. Prayers of thanksgiving lifted.

I told both children how much I loved them, and planted butterfly kisses by leaning close enough to let my eyelashes tickle their cheeks. Jessica laughed and Christopher smiled, both at the kiss and at her laughter, I think. Finally, I kissed Christopher and told him goodnight before Clara carried him to his bed. Hand in hand, Jessica and I went to her room where she'd be tucked cozy into her covers. Then the house was peaceful until the next sunrise.

When bedtime came for me, I called Jack into my room and put down his bed on the floor. He'd quickly come hopping into the bedroom, around the corner, and right into his own bed. He snuggled against his covers. I'd place a blanket over his body, and put his banana beside his head. I still couldn't find his dragon toy, but he seemed okay if he at least had his toy banana next to him.

Then I'd say, "I love you, beagle!" And I'd climb into bed, turn off the light, and hold my hand down to touch his head. We'd both sleep.

Two weeks before Halloween, Christopher lost his first tooth at the age of six years old.

The night before Halloween the children donned their handmade Halloween costumes and we headed to a community festival. Christopher dressed as a dinosaur and Jessica as the cutest witch. My little dinosaur won the contest for best costume.

While pulling Jack's blanket over his body on that chilly autumn night, I noticed the lump on the inside of his back left leg. The raised place was only as wide as the pad on my pinkie finger and barely noticeable, but I'd checked that same spot twice a week since Jack's radiation. To me, the growth certainly signaled cancer's return. At the vet's office the next morning, he confirmed it was obvious to him too.

The vet solemnly asked if he should refer Jack back to the oncologist, but I declined that referral. I already knew I wouldn't put Jack through any more radiation or surgery. On the graduation day of his radiation treatments, I'd made him a promise, a promise not forgotten. Never again would my beagle need to be so brave and strong.

Now it was my turn to be brave and strong.

The vet said Jack might live for a few months, maybe until Christmas if we were lucky. Last time Jack's cancer diagnosis meant grueling trips for radiation that gave him more time, but at a cost of his pain and fear. This time he deserved every opportunity for days filled with every pleasure he loved. He chased his tennis balls and munched on favorite treats. He rode with me through the drive-in for vanilla ice cream.

One sunny morning, I put the top down in my convertible and fastened Jack into the passenger's seat. Jack had ridden with me many times, but never with the top down because I'd thought he would be afraid. When the open car began moving, Jack sank into the seat a little. As the car picked up speed, he lifted his head into the wind, beagle ears flapping. Yes, he loved it! I wished I'd taken him on a hundred other convertible rides.

A few days later we took the convertible out to the family farm so Jack could ride in a pickup truck down a dirt country road. I held him in the back, propped on the side of the truck's bed so he could experience the feeling dogs seem to love of having their heads out a window. At first he was hesitant, but then the wind began to blow through my hair and his beagle hound dog ears lifted in the wind. Oh yes, he loved that ride too. I wished I'd taken him on a million other rides in the back of trucks.

Every day we spent as much time as possible cuddling and eating treats and playing. He wallowed in freshly-washed blankets every day. He ate his favorite foods at every meal. He chased balls and chewed up new toys.

I wondered if he knew he was dying. I wished I didn't know.

The tumor grew bigger with each passing day. In the moments I could face the inevitable, I began to research options for Jack's last day. Somewhere I'd heard about a service that sent trained professionals into homes to provide euthanasia to dying pets. I knew I didn't want the experience Ozzie had at the local emergency animal hospital. The people there were wonderful, but we were not at home.

If any dog deserved to die at home, my Jack did. He'd had to suffer and wait too long to have his forever home, and he'd be so afraid if we had to go somewhere, anywhere else. No, he was going to die at home if I could at all manage it.

Only three weeks after I knew Jack's cancer returned, the tumor grew too large and a blood vessel burst, turning Jack's leg black and purple. The on-call vet's technician acknowledged the broken vessel might be painful for him. She warned that even if the blood dissipated, it would happen again. The end was coming too quickly.

That same afternoon Jack stood at the back door and barked to let me know he wanted to go outside. The weather was sunny and warm, a perfect autumn day. Jack did something he'd never done because of his fears of the outdoors: he stretched out on the deck and stayed. I walked out to take his picture, resting so calmly in the sunshine's warmth. Then I saw the yellow butterfly, flitting across the yard toward Jack. He didn't move as it flew closer to him, and then danced in the air all around him. When the butterfly flew away, Jack stood to go back inside.

The next morning I frantically spent time on the telephone trying to reach the service advertising their end-of-life care for family pets, but they could not come until the next week. I felt panicked, not wanting to wait too long and have Jack suddenly become too ill.

That afternoon Jack again asked to go outside. Again he rested calmly in the sunshine. And again the butterfly came.

Early the next morning, I answered the phone to hear a familiar voice from the vet's office. The technician gave me bittersweet news: our family's own vet, the doctor who'd treated Jack for all those years, would come the next morning and help with Jack's transformation. I cried tears of gratitude and tears of sorrow.

That afternoon, for the third time, Jack went outside, stretched out in the sunshine, and waited. Soon the yellow butterfly danced all around him. When it left, he came back inside.

The butterfly never returned.

Sleep happened in only a few fitful hours that night. I didn't want to sleep at all, for I wanted every second with my beagle. Around 4 a.m. I moved from the bedroom to the couch in the living room and Jack moved out of his bed to follow me. He went up the steps to the couch and lay at the couch's end. I stretched out beside him there, my toes in socks touching his paws. How I longed for time to stand still with my beagle beside me! As daylight came, I cooked him eggs with cheese, one of his favorites, and gave him dog cookies.

Around 10 a.m. the vet and his intern rang the doorbell. Jack's bed lay ready in the living room, a special handmade quilt, freshly laundered, topping the bed. The kitchen counter's radio played peaceful instrumental music as we took our places on the floor surrounding Jack. I shared a few of my beagle's life stories; we laughed about how he ate my students' papers and lamented his lifelong fears.

Finally the room grew silent. I nodded my consent. When my veterinarian friend administered the injection, I swear to you the radio began to play "Somewhere Over the Rainbow." Jack, so strong to the end, stayed with us longer than I thought he would, but finally he succumbed to the drug's power to transform.

I put my arms around my sweet, brave hound one last time and whispered to him words I knew were true. The vet lovingly wrapped Jack in his favorite quilt with his banana toy, as requested. Then he carried my beagle's body away.

Both children turned up their noses at my spaghetti sauce for supper, but devoured the chocolate pudding. We made music around the piano, watched an episode of Alf, read a story, and folded wee hands in prayers. I kissed Christopher goodnight and Clara carried him to his bedroom before she left. In Jessica's room, I read her "Go Dogs Go." At her insistence, we read it again. Then I tucked her in and the day was done.

I awoke early the next morning and already was on my second cup of coffee and talking on the phone to a friend when Clara came through the door. I smiled and waved to her, as she headed straight upstairs to Christopher's room so she could bring him down for our breakfast together. Five minutes passed, maybe ten, before she walked back down the stairs alone and stood in front of me without speaking. I asked my friend to hold on a moment.

"Is everything OK?" Clara began shaking her head from side to side.

Then she whispered in a strange, small voice, "He's gone."

Without saying another word, I pushed the "off" button on the phone and ran to Christopher's room. Still in his bed, his covers turned down, his head on the white pillowcase, he was not moving. His face had no color; his lips seemed blue. I put my hands on either side of his cheeks, and his body felt warm to me.

Not stone-cold dead, my mind shouted. Still warm.

I called his name, tried to get him to breathe, begged him to breathe. I yelled downstairs, telling Clara to call 911.

Still my boy didn't move. Not breathing. Sirens coming closer and closer. Down the street, into my drive. Sounds of strangers running into the house, up the steps. My baby boy. Not breathing. Too still.

The emergency technicians ran into Christopher's room, one person firmly guiding me away from his bed and out of the room. I clutched the banister with both hands and forced myself to move down the steps. Clara still stood with my daughter beside her in the middle of the living room. Clara's face registered her shock. Jessica, clutching Clara's hand, seemed terrified. I raised my voice to Clara, demanding she get Jessica out of the house, to sit with her in the car outside.

I stood in the living room alone then, listening to the strangers in the room above me, as they tried to save my son. In minutes that seemed like hours, they brought Christopher down on a stretcher. "We were able to restart his heart, but we're not certain about his condition." They told me they were heading to the nearest hospital, about five minutes away.

Still in my bathrobe and slippers, I went to my room and quickly put on clothes. I remember standing in front of my bathroom vanity with a brush in my hand, looking into the mirror, and saying aloud to the pale woman there, "Why does it matter if you brush your hair?"

On my way to the car, I told Jessica I loved her and hugged both her and Clara before leaving for the hospital. I don't remember driving there, but recall parking my car, hurrying through the emergency room lobby, and following a doctor back to a consultation room. Already he'd examined Christopher, but he questioned me about my son's medical history. He asked if he could call our pediatrician, so I gave him the phone number. I waited, wondering when I could see my child, wondering why he was calling the doctor back home.

When the physician returned, he explained he'd wanted to speak to my son's regular doctor because of Christopher's "special condition." He said our pediatrician indicated I'd want him to do anything for my son that any parent would want done, regardless of Christopher's disabilities. I don't know why people didn't understand that without being told.

The doctor said he was sending Christopher to the pediatric intensive care team at the much larger Charleston hospital. A helicopter would fly my son there. Again, he left me alone to make arrangements. Soon he returned, apologizing that they could not send him by helicopter as they usually would because the helicopter had been called to the scene of a bad car accident. We'd travel by ambulance instead, and I could ride with them in the front passenger seat. As he hurriedly ushered me out to the ambulance where uniformed personnel were loading Christopher's stretcher into the back, he said they usually didn't allow passengers. I thanked him for his kindness.

I wish I could forget that ambulance ride. I tried to pretend I was anywhere but in an ambulance carrying my little boy.

My view out the wide front windows looked like any ordinary day's drive on the four-lane highway between vacation destinations. A sunny cruise between beaches by families packed into SUVs with luggage racks atop, sports cars with blaring radios and booming bass, big rigs carrying heavy loads to their next stops. Traffic as usual, until the drivers looked up into their rearview mirrors to see our vehicle's flashing red lights and the "AMBULANCE" across our windshield.

Then careful, considerate drivers quickly signaled and pulled into the right lane. Others panicked at our approach, abruptly jerking their steering wheel, throwing dust from the road's side as their cars left the pavement. Some drivers didn't move quickly enough or at all, until the ambulance driver switched on the siren's sound to force their move. Those drivers I inwardly cursed, for that delay of even seconds, but also for the siren's terrifying reminder to me that this was no joy ride.

Each time the siren wailed, I glanced over my left shoulder where two medical staff bent over the stretcher. Sometimes they called out numbers from the monitor. Occasionally they spoke to personnel at the Charleston unit, updating them on Christopher's condition, preparing for our arrival. Nobody spoke to me.

When the ambulance arrived at the hospital's emergency entrance, the attendants rushed to open the back door, jumped out, and rolled Christopher's stretcher through doors that shut behind them. I don't remember walking into the building, completing any registration or paperwork, or talking to anybody there for several hours. I know I paced alone in the long hallway of a waiting area, knowing doctors somewhere in that hospital worked to save my son. I called my family so some would care for Jessica and others be with me.

Finally the attending doctor called me back to the pediatric intensive care unit. As we walked to Christopher's location, he cautioned me about my son's condition. Yes, his vital signs were stable, but the respirator enabled him to breathe. And they did not yet know the damage done to his brain during the period when he was not breathing. The doctor explained he would run two sets of scans to determine brain wave activity, and then he'd meet with me again.

I stood beside Christopher's side for a few moments, touching his forehead and his hands carefully. Machines surrounded him, beeping their warnings, breathing for him. Needles and wires protruded from every limb. He was still, so still, moving only with the machines. I leaned down to kiss his cheek. I couldn't smell his usual sweet aroma's blend of bath-time lotion. I smelled sterile tape and alcohol and my own fear.

I left the intensive care unit and waited. Through the afternoon, the evening, the darkness of a night without our bedtime ritual I loved.

Dawn came, twenty-four hours after the morning I'd last held him in his room. The doctor called to me from the waiting area and led me back to where Christopher had spent the night without me. As I approached the small hospital bed, I had a flashback of the first time I ever saw my son. I put my hand over his little one, listening to the doctor's report of two scans, both showing no brain activity.

That doctor took my other hand, holding it while he told me he believed Christopher had died peacefully in his own little bed. Only the machines kept him breathing, his heart beating. He'd never be able to do those things on his own again. In a quiet voice I didn't recognize as my own, I asked the doctor if Christopher's organs could be used for another child, but he said that wasn't possible. I listened as the doctor kindly told me he could tell Christopher had wonderful care, that he knew how much I loved my son. Long after that conversation, I recalled his words and wondered if he knew the inevitable guilt felt by parents whose children die.

With a heavy sigh, the doctor explained what would happen next. When I gave the hospital my consent and signed the necessary papers, they would remove the respirator, monitors, and machines. Then they'd bring Christopher into a private room where I could be with him as long as I wanted. "Could you remove his gastrostomy tube too so I can hold him closer?" I asked. I'd never stopped hating that tube. The doctor said, "Of course."

I kissed Christopher's forehead again and walked out of the unit.

Soon a nurse called my name and led me to a small room bright with the morning's sunlight. A large wooden rocking chair waited. I sat down as the doctor carried in my boy, placing Christopher in my arms. As I began to rock, I thought about how the first time I held Christopher and the last time I held him, we rocked. I pulled him closer on my lap, his precious head in the crook of my left arm, his beautiful face I so loved against me, the way I always held him. I wanted to sing to him, but no sound would come out of me.

So I rocked him in silence until I no longer felt the air leaving his body as if he were sighing to be free.

Part II

After Life

Chapter 7: The Journey

"If only I had known." People often say that phrase after a loved one dies, and then they go on to tell us something they'd have done differently. They would have telephoned their parent more often. They'd have visited an uncle, or written a letter to their sister. They would have said "I'm sorry" to a former friend.

"If only I had known," we lament while in the hospital emergency room, at the funeral home, or beside a grave. Especially beside a grave.

Sometimes I hear those words, and almost shout out, "We know! We <u>always</u> know!"

We absolutely know we will die. So will all those whom we dearly love. (And so will those we don't like at all, although it sometimes feels as if, unfairly, they live longer.) We know! Death comes to all.

No cure exists for death. Ashes-to-ashes is a kept promise.

Of course what we really mean is, "If only I had known exactly when death would happen." If only we knew the moment death would occur – our own or our loved ones' passing. Sometimes we do know approximately when death will arrive, if a loved one has suffered a long illness. We watch death coming.

I've stood with families when the death of a loved one was near. We'd each silently count the seconds between the inhalations, holding our own breaths between the pauses. The rise of a breath, the fall. The rise, the fall, until the breaths stop.

More often though, we are sincerely shocked by death's impertinent, inconvenient, often inconceivable arrival, especially when death comes too early. Family members were not ready for the news when my great-grandfather sat down in the middle of his vegetable garden and died, even though he'd lived 89 years. The more jolting shock comes when a 45-year-old professor dies from her first heart attack an hour after teaching a class, or when a 32-year-old father succumbs to a brain aneurysm, or when a 24-year-old doesn't live after a car crash.

Or when a six-year-old child dies in his bed one November morning.

I'm not certain whether knowing in advance matters in the end, but the preliminary knowledge does alter the beginning of the grieving process. Perhaps we grieve no less deeply when we expect death to happen, but we begin the journey differently.

When Christopher died without warning, I had no time for advance grief and no preparations of heart and spirit. Although he'd almost died at birth and again when he suffered cardiac arrest at three-years-old, he'd had relatively stable health for a couple of years. He was not sick in the weeks or months before he died. I had absolutely no thought of his death when I kissed him goodnight the evening before he stopped breathing. And then he was gone.

Christopher died in his own little bed, the kind doctor said, but I wasn't there beside him. That stranger in his white coat, who officially proclaimed the time of Christopher's death on the next day, tried to assure me that death had not happened there in the intensive care unit while my child lay amidst medical monitors, or in the terrifying ambulance ride with sirens wailing. That doctor tried to comfort me with a more palatable story of how my son died all snuggled into his bed with the dinosaur sheets.

While I understand the medical process of Christopher's brain's death that morning, likely from a seizure, and while I remain grateful for the doctor's kindness, I don't know if my little boy felt pain or if he struggled or how he felt. I wasn't there with him. I can't know.

Death of our animal companions can break our hearts too. Our furry friends, including my beagle, also become our family members. Their deaths bring us grief as certainly as the loss of non-furry family. We mourn their passing as deeply, sometimes more deeply, than human companions.

With Jack's death, I'd lived with my concern and even grief for a long time. In going through his weeks of radiation treatments, I had to face his cancer head-on. Then every recheck held an element of fear as to whether his cancer had returned. My pre-grief then, for Jack, lasted for many months.

When the final tumor on his leg was evident, I knew the end was inevitable, and with no more than a couple of months at best. "Christmas," said the vet with hope. Instead, I had barely a month with my beagle. With Jack's death, I knew the tumor had returned. I knew he had only a short time, although I thought I'd have a month or two instead of just weeks. Then during his final 24 hours, I knew exactly how much time I had left with him.

Knowing that death approached him, I used our time together in the best possible way. In those last weeks, we rode in the back of a pickup truck and in my convertible. I cooked his favorite foods and we played his favorite games. I cherished every possible moment to snuggle with him. I took lots of photographs, including images of his paintbrush tail and his wide front paw and the heart on his head. In the last hours, I cuddled with him, just the two of us, on the couch, fed him scrambled eggs, and talked to him incessantly with words of love.

Knowing death's time, I carefully and lovingly planned his last moments. He died peacefully, surrounded by people he trusted, with soft music playing and his yellow banana toy next to him. He died with the freshly laundered blanket he loved best in his own bed. He died hearing my voice speak of my love for him.

With Jack's death, I knew death was near. With Christopher's death, I did not know.

If only I had known that Christopher would die on that morning, I would have done some things differently.

Maybe I even could have saved him? Perhaps if I had gone upstairs to his room when I first awoke that morning, I could have prevented his death. Maybe if I called 911 a moment earlier? If I could have started him breathing again before the EMT sirens sounded? Maybe?

In the journey of grief, it's the "maybe" thoughts that slay us.

If only I had known…even if I could not save him, I wish I could have held him. Especially I wish I'd been the one to tuck him into his bed that night. To hold him for a few moments longer before he slept. Or at least to find him the next morning, to spare Clara that heartbreak.

Knowing death will come and yet not knowing when, we can't always have the exact endings we wish. The lesson – one I must remind myself over and over when I feel guilt: *If we humans love and live the best we can with the knowledge we have at the time, that's the best we can live our lives.*

I try then to find peace by reminding myself that in the hours before he died, I did the best I could to love my son. I performed things I'd done every day since his birth: prepared his meals and measured out his medicines; pushed his wheelchair outside for him to hear the ocean's song and feel salty breezes on his cheeks; intertwined our fingers so he could finger-paint a rainbow; sang silly songs at the piano; read a favorite book; and kissed him goodnight.

Most importantly, I loved him. And I told him I loved him. Every day. Sometimes every hour. At the moment Christopher died, I know he knew I loved him. I didn't get to speak the words in his last moment, as I did with Jack, but I know he knew.

Death's timing, whether we know it's approaching or whether it sneaks in as the thief, affects not only our regrets about the moments of death, but also how our grief journey begins and evolves.

With Jack's death, I'd already spent time in a state of pre-grief. I knew his death was coming, and soon. Before his last breath, I already had begun to grieve. So when Jack died, I did not experience a period of shock, but instant intense grief. I watched the vet carry my beagle's body out of the front door, and immediately felt the depths of my loss.

When Christopher died, I instead went into a stage of shock. Nothing penetrated the numbness of that armor. No feelings. Probably the shock began at home when I first saw his lifeless body, but certainly I didn't identify my state of shock until long after that initial stage of grief passed.

I now know shock enabled me to function during those first hours. How else could I have ridden silently in the front seat of my son's ambulance without screaming at cars to move out of the way, or climbing over the front seat to hold my child? Would not only shock allow me to write a poem about my son on the night before his burial? Wasn't shock the only thing keeping me breathing after my child took his last breath?

Certainly shock empowered me to walk out of the hospital after I'd handed my child's body over to the doctor. At the time I didn't realize anything about my condition, but later I clearly recognized the signs. I remember my family members, knowing I hadn't eaten that day, suggesting we stop to eat in the city before beginning the trip home. I walked into a restaurant with them, ordered from the menu, and ate my lunch as if my son's body was not in a hospital morgue.

I don't recall all of the details from the next few days after Christopher's death, but I functioned through those early days and weeks without feeling anything except fatigue. I somehow packed my clothes and my daughter's to travel the four hours from the beach back to home. Family members handled the burial arrangements while I planned two gatherings, one at the children's center as a celebration of Christopher's life, and the other as a time for receiving family and friends in our church's fellowship hall.

Shock was my protector, my friend. Unbelievably to me in later weeks, I ate and spoke without emotion, without crying, in those first days. I drove my car and cared for my daughter. I even slept. But when I awoke, my first thought before opening my eyes would be, "Christopher died."

I participated in death's rituals with ease. At the event planned to visit with friends and family in the church fellowship hall, I displayed favorite photographs to share Christopher's life. I'd not allowed an open casket except for immediate family's viewing, but wanted to share his childhood with anyone who came to pay their respects. Even at the receiving, I recall people coming by and speaking to me, but don't remember crying hysterically as perhaps they expected. We carried on conversations as if gathering at a grocery store instead of a building 50 yards from my boy's open grave site.

For the private children's center celebration, I'd purchased plants for my family, friends, and the center's staff to place in the garden outside the facility's common area. While planting trees in Christopher's memory, I wore a black sweatshirt featuring a bright white image of my second favorite beagle, Snoopy. Somehow I thought I would feel joy from putting a tree into the ground at the same moment my son's body was being lowered into the ground at a cemetery 20 minutes away. Instead, I felt nothing because shock protected me. I couldn't bear the thought of being graveside during that precious little body's burial. I can't bear the thought of it still.

With my mourning delayed by shock, I didn't experience the loss of Christopher's presence at all in those first days or for a long time after his death. So strange then, when I remember how I immediately and deeply felt my dog, Jack's absence. I cried inconsolably in the hours after he died. I didn't eat. I didn't want to talk with family and friends.

Grief's sharpest pain from my beagle's death came with nightfall on his death day. Remember, our bedtime ritual since adoption was that I'd announce bedtime for everyone and then, when I was in my bedroom, I'd carry Jack's bed from the room's corner to the place right beside the bed. He slept close beside me where I could touch him, if needed, for his comforting through the night. I loved being able to drop my arm off the bed and find his soft fur within my reach.

On the night of his death, I looked at his bed in that corner and began crying. Then I said aloud, "Jack, I know heaven is much more fun but I need you to come back with me, just at night, for a little while."

I put his bed down in its usual place, got into bed myself, turned out the light on the night stand, and waited for only a few moments before he came to me. In my room. Into his bed.

No, his body didn't return. Instead I felt a sense of peace filling the room, and then Jack's sweet presence as surely as when he'd hopped into his bed the night before. I believe with all of my heart Jack was back there beside me.

That first night passed calmly, peacefully, after he came. I slept soundly. Early the next morning as the sun barely began to rise, I awoke and opened my eyes. I heard a voice – inside my head, not aloud, but no less certainly than if I'd heard it with my ears. Jack said, "Ozzie said to tell you: in heaven, dogs can eat chocolate."

Jack's spirited presence left me during the days, but returned each night when I placed his bed beside mine. Gradually over the next few weeks, Jack's presence, I sensed, was not with me throughout all the night. And then not at all.

So many decisions are necessary after the death of someone we love. Sometimes we've planned ahead, but often we make those decisions in the midst of sorrow or during the stage of shock. The customs for burial or cremation are often different for people and animals, but there are similarities.

I never spent much time in the cemetery of the church where I grew up until after Christopher died. I'd never given any thought to where I'd want my children to be buried because – well, who plans for the deaths of their children? When Christopher died, I knew I needed his body close to someone else's who loved him. Thankfully, the church had the perfect cemetery plot available.

While I was pregnant with Jessica, my grandmother, Mama Ree, died. (We grandchildren heard our parents call her "Mama," while others called her by her name, Marie. So we called her "Mama Ree.") Mama Ree would tell you she didn't have favorites when it came to her children or her grandchildren, but then she'd smile coyly to me and say, "But now Christopher, he's special." She loved her great-grandson well. She held him and rocked him at home and on her visits to the children's center.

Mama Ree died much too early, and I don't understand why. However, I do believe she was waiting on Christopher in heaven and sometimes I think maybe that's why she went there far too soon. When Christopher died, I wanted his body to be as close as possible to hers. So he was buried with his grave plot in front of hers in a family section of the church cemetery.

Jack has no cemetery plot with a stone marker. When Jack died, I already had experience with our other dogs and cats being cremated and didn't hesitate when I needed to decide for Jack's body. My vet's office called a few days after my beagle's death, letting me know Jack's remains were there.

Now a shelf in the living room holds a small wooden box with his ashes, alongside containers with the ashes of Patches, Ozzie, and Dodger. Someday I'll be strong enough to release Jack's ashes into an ocean breeze. Not yet.

One of the strangest parts of a survivor's journey after the death of a loved one is that death doesn't stop life for the rest of humanity. Someone dies, we grieve, and everyone else lives on. We mourners feel as if the world certainly should be changed by our loss. Yet all around us, life goes on as if nothing happened. Traffic lights still turn from green to yellow to red. Telephones ring. Gardens grow. The sun rises and sets.

After Christopher's burial, I returned to the beach where life existed for everyone else just as if he'd never lived or died. Still in shock, I moved with the rest of the world for several weeks. I ate and slept and walked on the beach and took Jess to playschool. I thought I was fine, although my body felt strangely numb, as if the entire body and spirit had been injected with a dentist's deadening agent. I didn't think about anything except the superficial decisions necessary to move us through each day.

Two early signs pointed to the devastating grief ahead, but I couldn't see the storm's approach. My first hint that I was not "Just fine," as I told family and friends who called, was my empty journal. I'd kept diaries and journals since the age of 10, but I didn't pick up a pen at all in those first weeks after Christopher's death. Even when I began journaling again, I certainly didn't write about his death or Jack's death, or, in fact, any other grief.

The other sign, a strange episode, should have been a certain clue of imminent grief. My daughter and I had been home only two days after Christopher's burial, and we needed groceries. Past the mall's stores, we walked and window-shopped until we reached the large anchor store selling everything from auto parts to shoes to the milk and bread we needed. As we entered the store, I turned my body slightly away from Jessica's to get a buggy. When I turned the buggy back around and looked down, she was gone.

For a few seconds, I stood paralyzed. Then the panic jolted me into action. I frantically looked around in every direction and couldn't see her. I dashed over to a cashier near the large opening that funneled shoppers back into the mall and told her I needed help, that I couldn't find my daughter, and that I was going to look for her. "Don't let any little girl go out of this store," I demanded.

As I started to turn away from the clerk to go back to searching, I stopped. I whirled around to face her, my voice shaking uncontrollably, and screamed, "My little boy died last week! I can't lose her too!"

I'd taken only a few steps away from the clerk when I noticed a circular rack of clothing holding tee shirts with beach names, and the little legs protruding beneath the shirts' hemlines. I called to her, as calmly as if we were playing hide-and-seek in the park, "Jessica, I found you." She came running out from beneath the clothes with glee. I took her tiny hand in mine, walked past the sales clerk, saying without emotion, "Thank you. I found her," and left the store for home.

Safely back at home, I asked Jessica never to hide from me again. Then we both had ice cream and I slept in her bed with her that night.

Sure, I was fine. "Just fine," I told everyone and I believed it. When a flicker of thought about

Christopher's death flashed, I'd tell myself he wasn't suffering now. I thought I was fine.

Shock's insulating barrier eventually fades, allowing grief's pain to break through. About a month after we'd returned to the beach, I drove to my favorite breakfast spot. I'd planned to linger over coffee and make notes for a newspaper article. As I sat alone in the booth awaiting a refill on my coffee, I barely noticed a group of three EMT personnel in uniform come through the door. I looked up from my paper with my pen still in hand, to see an ambulance parked outside in the restaurant's parking lot.

The two men and one woman sat at a table twenty feet across the room from me. I couldn't hear their conversation, but every once in a while, I heard their laughter. Hot coffee sloshed in the chipped mug between my trembling hands. I glanced out the window where they'd parked the ambulance, vaguely noticing its familiar markings. I couldn't seem to get my breath. When I tried to put down the mug, I noticed my arms, my whole body, felt heavy as if I couldn't move.

They laughed again. I looked down to see a salty puddle pooling in what had been my empty plate. I hadn't realized I'd been crying. Just then my server stopped beside my table, noticed my tears, and asked if she could help. She called a cab to give me a ride home.

With that episode, my shock ended and I began to feel the pain. At first, the sensation of grief felt dull, like anesthesia fading, allowing subtle aches of sorrow. I'd open a kitchen cabinet and wince as I noticed the blender I no longer needed to make Christopher's meals. I'd walk down the beach past the place where the children met a multitude of seagulls, and take the street route back home so I wouldn't need to pass that spot again.

Soon after, the nightmares began. I'd dream of ambulance rides in which I knew the attendants were working with my boy in the back, but cars in front of us wouldn't move aside, despite the blaring sirens and flashing lights. Or I'd dream of hospital hallways. I'd search, but couldn't find him. From those nightmares, I would awaken and he still was gone. I grew afraid of going to sleep.

A friend suggested I try going to a support group. I remember sitting in a circle of people, parents of various ages. The first person speaking told a detailed story about her teenaged son killing himself at their home. I could tell she'd told that story there before. Other parents in the circle nodded politely, expressed their compassion. I thought I'd scream. My chest muscles hurt. I thought I would not live to get out of that room. When the group took a break for lemonade and cookies, I fled the building and never went back.

Since returning to the beach house after Christopher's burial, I hadn't been upstairs to his room. After the restaurant incident, I would wake up in the morning and sit in the living area with my coffee, looking up at the steps. Some mornings I would believe for a while that, if I'd go up those stairs, I'd find him in his bed as if nothing ever happened. Some mornings I thought I heard sounds that could have been his vocalizations. Some mornings I believed he was there, but I didn't want to go up so I could continue believing he might be alive. Some mornings I thought I was crazy.

To the world around me, I likely still looked sane. I'd shop for groceries. I'd take my little girl to the park or a movie. I partitioned my emotions, attempting to protect my daughter. While she played at preschool, I'd allow myself to think briefly about Christopher.

Most of the time I functioned normally because I kept the emerging pain pushed down inside. No, I'd admit I wasn't "fine" anymore, but I could handle this.

Meanwhile, the sorrow grew stronger with every nightmare, with every daydream. I'd hear a siren and begin to weep. I'd see a distant glimpse of parents pushing their child in a wheelchair toward me at the mall, and I'd escape to the parking lot where I'd sit trembling for hours before I could drive back home.

I didn't want to sleep because of the nightmares. Every dream brought jolting images of hospital hallways or ambulance rides. I didn't want to be awake either.

Finally my nighttime peace returned after a vision from my grandmother, Mama Ree. In a dream, I was talking to my Granddaddy when Mama Ree appeared in the room. From his lack of reaction, I knew he didn't see her so I waited until he left and then I spoke to her.

"Mama Ree, why couldn't Granddaddy see you?"

"Because he didn't need to see me. I came to see you."

I couldn't help but stare at her. Somehow her features looked the same as the last time I saw her before her death, but she also appeared more beautiful than I'd ever seen any human look, as if she glowed from the inside. I told her so.

"In heaven, we get to choose how we look. I felt comfortable looking like my last self," she said with a laugh. "I came to tell you about Christopher. He's in his twenties here, but still so handsome and with those long eyelashes. Most importantly, he wants you to know he's okay."

Then she disappeared. I opened my eyes, and I never had another bad dream about Christopher.

Many friends and most acquaintances didn't stay in contact after Christopher's death, but I take the blame for the loss of relationships. I preferred, at least subconsciously, to stay away from people who knew Christopher. Sharing the grief was too heavy a burden.

Occasionally friends and family would come to visit with me as before, enjoying our proximity to the beach. Yet now I tried my best to keep them away because I couldn't predict whether I could manage to hide my emerging emotions. And when loved ones did visit me, our conversations felt uncomfortable or stifled.

Nobody knows exactly what to say to a parent who's lost her or his child, or to anyone grieving the loss of someone they love. The truth is there are no perfect words to comfort us, but I can tell you a few things not to say. Please don't tell me I'm more special for having this experience. Don't try to convince me that the death is Godde's will or assure me my child is better off now.

Don't flinch if you're with me when a stranger asks "Do you have children?" and I respond, "Two children," when you know one is dead. And don't judge me if I answer them, "One," because I can't bear to explain why my little girl is playing beside me and my son is not.

Please don't tell me the first year after a loved one's death is the worst. And don't you dare say, or even imply, that the time has passed, enough time, for me to be over my grieving unless you can bring my little boy back from the dead.

Yet, I beg you, please don't go away.

Instead of sending flowers that die more quickly than I can arrange a burial, send me a card a month later. Call me three months past his death when most people have forgotten my loss. Visit me six months, a year, after his funeral. Please don't give up on me.

And while the words don't exist that will remove my heartache, your compassionate presence will bring me comfort. Please be with me in my silence, or listen well when I want to talk about my child. Do remember his birthday. Please do send a note or call me on his death date.

Keep my beloved in your heart too. Let his photograph stay in your wallet or on your mantle. Tell me a story you recall about him.

Remember his life, the way he taught us more about love than any poet or preacher or philosopher. Love him still.

Two months before the first anniversary of Christopher's death, a hurricane hit the beach in an almost-direct strike. I drove away from our home at midnight, prior to a forced evacuation already ordered for the next day. I packed no clothes, but loaded the car with all of my photo albums and every single one of Christopher's music boxes. When I returned to the beach a few days after the storm, the house was intact but the town suffered in the aftermath. Debris littered the beaches. Piers I'd visited since childhood were gone. Bulldozers moved sand from main roads.

The devastation outside the beach house intensified the panic I felt as Christopher's death date approached. I began to realize I had to leave that house. Two weeks before his death date, I loaded up the last of my and my daughter's belongings, and said goodbye to the house where my little boy died.

Time passed. The adage, "Time heals all wounds," is not true. The debilitating all-consuming grief had subsided, but in its place came grief more difficult because of its unpredictable nature. At some moments, I could smile and even laugh, but then I'd remember I'd suffered great loss. Grief would appear at unexpected and inconvenient moments. I had no control. Some wounds scab over, but then life knocks off the scab and the wound oozes again.

Anniversary dates were like that for me. Holidays and birthdays, joyous occasions before, became burdensome. People told me the first year's cycle of holidays would be the most difficult, but I stayed in the shock stage of grief long enough to celebrate the first Christmas and birthday without a significant struggle.

Christmas Day arrived six weeks after my child's graveside marker's placement. Already, before his death, I'd bought Christopher two gifts: a book of poetry and a musical instrument. When I placed Ms. Santa's gifts for Jessica around the tree on Christmas Eve, I put those gifts out too for my son. A small lighted tree stood beside his cemetery stone.

On his first birthday after Christopher's death, I didn't get to sing to him or to bake a cake topped with seven candles. Instead, I wrote a message on a piece of paper, attached it to balloons, stood in the cemetery, and sent his balloon bouquet to heaven. I watched the balloons lift past trees, past buildings, until I could barely make out a spot in the far away sky. Then I couldn't see them anymore, so I knew he had them in heaven. Every year since his death, I've sent him balloons with a birthday love note.

On Jack's first birthday after his death, I'd gone back to the beach, thinking I'd recapture the peace I once knew there. Instead, I felt deep loss as soon as I arrived. The drive was too long and difficult for me to return home that night, so I decided to wait until the next morning. The day had been sad and stressful. I lamented how I'd even forgotten to pack chocolate, my favorite comfort food.

The next morning, Jack's birthday, I awoke feeling deep grief as I prepared to leave. While straightening the kitchen, I wanted to find a good place to put a package of new batteries bought to use for the television remote. I walked into the main bedroom and opened the nightstand.

There was Jack's dragon toy! Missing for over a year! Someone found that shabby toy, stiff from dog drool, and, miraculously, did not throw it in the trash.

I held that old toy close to me. For a moment, I could sense Jack's presence back with me. Then I felt him say, "A birthday present for you."

Instantly, joy replaced my grief. I believe I danced through the rest of my packing. When I popped open the trunk of the car to load my suitcase, I saw the bar of dark chocolate in the middle of the trunk as if it'd been carefully placed there. Immediately I again heard Jack's voice in my head, "And Ozzie sent you chocolate."

Jack's birthday, celebrated on the day of his adoption, remains in my calendar. Each year my beagle's birthday is observed with special treats to my other animal companions, with a donation to a dog rescue, and with a birthday song to the heavens.

Anniversary dates of their deaths remained difficult. Those days made me sad, especially Christopher's death date. Each year I'd begin to feel grief when Halloween decorations appeared in stores, remembering he wore his dinosaur costume two weeks before he died. After Halloween, I'd become sadder with each passing day until I awoke with the crushing awareness that his death date had arrived. Every anniversary morning, I'd opened my eyes with a flashback, as if Christopher were still in a room upstairs, still in his bed, still not breathing.

Twice on Christopher's death date I landed in a hospital's emergency room with crushing chest pains, afraid I might be having a heart attack. After ruling out heart issues with an EKG and x-ray, the physician would ask, "Is there anything in your life that might be causing you stress?"

"Well, today happens to be the date on which my little boy died when he was six."

A broken heart is a real diagnosis. No cure.

The worst wounds didn't always wait for holidays and anniversaries. Ordinary days could unexpectedly stab me in the heart. I'd see someone walking a lemon beagle down the street. Or a family would enter a restaurant with a child in the blue wheelchair. Or anyone could start singing "You Are My Sunshine." Open wounds again.

I believe in an After Life. I've lost some tenets of my childhood faith through education, life experiences, and my personal transformation in an understanding of the Holy One. Yet never once has my faith in resurrected life faltered. I believe. My belief is no longer based on a child's Sunday School lessons or a teenager's desperate search for personal spiritual meaning or a middle-aged seminarian's academic research. I believe.

My personal belief now is strengthened by what I testify as proof: my own visions in voice and dreams and even sightings. These spiritual experiences bring me hope and joy. (If you believe differently, I'm not trying to convince you or proselytize. I wish only peace and healing for you as you seek your own answers.)

In heaven, I think we'll appear to others in whatever form we choose. When I go to heaven, I can choose to house my spirit in my 10-year-old body that held the pen writing my first diary. Or I can choose to fly above clouds in the body of an eagle – if I lose my fear of heights in heaven. I can appear as a purple butterfly in one moment, and as my silver-haired self the next.

I know this about heaven because, as I've shared, my Mama Ree told me. She'd never tell a lie, much less a lie about heaven. Plus she would know because she was there when she told me. Remember the dream I shared with you? In heaven now, Christopher gets to choose how he looks. In the dream where Mama Ree told me my son was happy, she told me he'd chosen to appear as a young man in his twenties.

When I was in my initial semester of seminary, I drove to campus for the first day of exams. I was exhausted from late-night studying, and anxious about the testing ahead. Deciding not to park in the remote lot with a long bus ride, I drove straight to a parking area nearest the seminary building. I circled through the lot and found not a single open space.

Feeling panicked, I decided I had no choice but to park in the paid section between Duke Chapel and the Student Center. I turned into the lot and thankfully saw one parking space remaining. I pulled in, quickly got out of the car with backpack in tow, and hurriedly stood before the parking meter. Pulling out my wallet, I realized I had none of the necessary coins, only three single one-dollar bills. Never one to break any rules, I stood there trying to decide if I could move my car and still make it to the classroom on time. No, I'd move my car, but likely would miss my first exam.

Then I saw the young man walking straight for me, his open palm outstretched in my direction. "Need some quarters," he asked? "Oh, yes! Thank you so much! I have dollars to trade you." He put the quarters into the parking meter. I turned to retrieve my dollars in exchange, voicing my gratitude as I gathered my money.

When I turned back to him, he was gone. I looked in every direction but saw nobody. I grabbed my book bag and began walking to class. Halfway to the exam room, I paused, took a deep breath, and said aloud, "Christopher gave me change."

In heaven now, my son gets to choose how he looks, Mama Ree said. The young man who helped me beside Duke Chapel looked just as my grandmother described: long eyelashes, gentle smile, strong body, in his 20s, kind, compassionate. I'll always believe Christopher visited me on exam day.

Heavenly dogs get to choose too, I believe. In heaven, I think my Jack still possesses those floppy hound-dog ears, his soft lemon-yellow fur, and, of course, the heart on his forehead. Only three legs still, though he runs and jumps and plays without difficulty.

The change my mind's eye sees for him: he's fearless. No more submissive posture. No one floppy ear always listening alert for scary noises. No cowering.

If heaven ever has fireworks, Jack dances and howls with delight at the sounds.

No fear. No wheelchairs. No sorrow. No illnesses. No cancer. No pain.

Free to be. Only Love.

When our loved ones die, what do we keep?

What remnants remain of Christopher's life? Shortly after his death, I sold some of Christopher's toys at a yard sale. I wasn't selling them because he died. Weeks before his death, I'd told family members I'd join them at a yard sale and already had gathered items. That Saturday morning I stood in a parking lot and held out a plastic fire fighter's hat to someone who knew me and Christopher. "Are you sure you want to sell that?" they asked when I mentioned it had belonged to him. "Yes, I'm glad your grandson will enjoy it. Please take it. No charge."

Two months later, when the initial shock began to fade, I cursed myself for letting go of that hat and of any item in my son's life. I could not even bear to part with a single item in Christopher's room. Family finally had to come to the beach and carry the furniture and belongings from his room. Before they removed his room's contents, I picked out what I needed to keep. His coat worn when Jessica was baptized, and his Christmas photograph outfits. His yellow lamb and quilt. Preschool love notes and cowboy boots.

His pajamas worn the night he'd died were the first thing I put aside. I held them closely to my face so I could breathe in the fragrance of my little boy. Two decades later, I unpacked a chest of memories and discovered those pajamas. Again, I held them against my cheek, closed my eyes, and tried to capture his aroma.

Of Jack's life, what do I have left? Two collars he wore. His scarf signed by the radiation team staff on his last day of treatments. Ashes in a box. A snippet of his fur. My shirt with which I covered him on his last night. His bed I continued to place beside mine every night for six months after his death.

My greatest treasures for both Christopher and Jack are my photographs that help me keep memories more vivid. My deepest emotions, as well as sensory triggers for those emotions, exist in those memories. In a state of intense emotion – falling in love, for example – we humans experience everyday events with a heightened sense of awareness, and, thus, the memories are etched more deeply. The difference in permanence seems like a light pencil stroke from a broken, shortened, dull pencil versus the penetrating steel-like metal point of a fountain pen dipped in indelible dark purple ink.

I don't want to forget one detail. I do recall many special moments from the significant days I spent with my son, and my beagle. To remember details from life events so important to me, while forgetting details of thousands of other days, is not surprising.

What is shocking to me though is the way grief connects the stories of those whom we love. Once I spoke aloud to someone about Jack's veterinarian and instead of his name, I spoke the name of my little boy's pediatrician.

Grief's threads weave tightly around every other grief.

As time passed, my grieving did not end, but it changed, of course. I understand well the experts' explanations of the grieving process. First, I lived in the extremes of those stages. After the initial shock – an eerie calm like the eye of a hurricane – then my body joined my brain in mourning. When the body's grief work (sobbing, failure to eat and sleep) was spent, the mind took control again and began to try processing. Sadness, anger, some acceptance. Finally the healing stage began when the physical and mental could rejoin.

Time is required for the body's parts to sync before any measure of healing may begin. Healing does not equal a removal of all pain or total restoration of what death took from me. Healing is the process of health's restoration, despite the continued pain and loss.

Healing is an interesting concept in religion, and a complex one, even in less dogmatic spirituality. In my religious tradition (from childhood), we prayed for people who were sick. At church, the pastor updated the congregation about people who were ill or facing surgery. The theological assumption is: we pray and Godde hears; Godde heals and people are well. As a child, I didn't experience significant loss so I had no personal reason to question the theology behind the church's directive and example of prayer for healing.

When Christopher was born – dead on arrival, but reborn again, albeit with serious medical needs – I didn't analyze that precept directly. I also didn't follow it. I feel certain I didn't blame Godde, but I also don't recall praying for my son to be healed. Probably I lifted prayers for his comfort or his eating or even a "normal" kind of recovery from a bout with pneumonia or a surgery. But I know I never prayed for a cure of his cerebral palsy or the long list of other disabilities.

A family member and I argued once because he wanted to take Christopher to a "faith healer" who was passing through town. My reasoning: if Godde intended to heal Christopher, then healing would happen without that stranger's intervention.

Did I ever, have I ever, prayed for physical healing since Christopher's birth? For anyone? I'm unsure. I know I've lifted countless prayers for loved ones and for strangers who were sick or injured. Yet my supplication for "healing" refers to a generic wholeness of peace and good and comfort.

When Jack's tumor came back, I recall trying an essential oil, gently rubbing it on the raised place on his leg. I don't remember uttering a prayer, but I'm sure I lifted up hope that the tumor would go away.

For Jack, I longed for his well-being, his peace, and his happiness. I never prayed for a new leg.

My omission of prayers traditionally considered "healing" connects with the bigger question of theodicy. I spent years considering (and later dissecting in seminary) the ancient question of "Why?" If, as I'd been taught from childhood on, Godde loved me (and everyone), and if Godde had the power to heal (and do everything), then why, oh why, would Godde allow a little boy to suffer as Christopher did? And then to die?

Now those were questions I did ask. Painfully, I realized too many others had asked the same questions before. Why?

But, on the other hand, why not me?

I grow uncomfortable when people enthusiastically rejoice at their survival from a disaster where others die, saying, "Thanks be to Godde for saving me!" Or when a critically ill person receives a good report from their medical tests and proclaims, "Prayers were answered," while a patient who sat beside them in the waiting room hears the opposite verdict. Did Godde not listen to them? Did their prayers fail?

I'm aware of credible medical research about prayers' influences, but I also know of instances when many good people were praying and a saint-of-a-person died. Bones and wounds often heal. Sometimes a threatening disease is cured. Sometimes not. Miracles happen all the time. Occasionally we stop to notice them.

I don't have the answers. I'm just asking the questions.

For my heart, I now choose to find peace in a question other than "Why?" Instead of continuing to agonize over the "why," I ask, "Where is Love?" In humanity's times of tragedy, where is Godde (the Holy One, the Creator, our Higher Power, in whatever name and imagery we humans use)? When I ask that question, I know my answer: the One who is perfect Love is with me. With me, in my joys and my sorrows.

I also choose to focus on an over-arching view of healing, the kind that lasts for always. When Jack was nearing his end, I saw the yellow butterfly and focused on transformation rather than calling for the disappearance of a tumor. Healing is a journey instead of the destination, just as long as we're in this world of potential heartache, illness, loneliness, pain, and death.

"I once was lost, but now I'm found…" are the words sometimes sung as people make their way from sitting in a hard pew to kneeling at an altar. In the days after Christopher's death – after the shock wore off in a few weeks or months, after time's passage shredded that blessed insulation with its protective padding between outright panic and elusive peace, between madness and maddening reality – I was lost.

Too lost to even know I was lost. I could breathe but only with shallow breaths, occasionally gasping from grief's chokehold. Knowing too deep a breath and I'd be suffocated by piercing pain. I could think, but only about the immediate reality in front of me. Not the past and certainly not a future.

Love saved me.

Love for my little girl, not quite three when her brother died, saved me. She held onto me tightly amidst my grief. She found me there. She still needed me. She still laughed and cried and sang and danced. She saved me.

Several months after her brother died, I tucked Jessica into her bed with her stuffed rabbit, Hop Hop, and read her a book or two. We'd commented on the glorious stars outside her window, but as we finished her prayers, a cloud passed by and the sky darkened.

"Oh no! The moon is gone!" Jessica cried out.

I gently, matter-of-factly, answered, "The moon is still there. We can't see it because the dark cloud's in the way, but the cloud will move and we'll see the light again."

Like death's darkness, I thought.

My love for her and hers for me saved me.

For days and weeks and months and years, I endured moments when the weight of grief threatened to crush me. In the middle of such a moment, my little girl would climb into my bed and grin as she asked, "What's for breakfast?" or "Will you read to me?" or "Let's play, Mommy!"

And then I'd live for another hour.

I lived through countless days when I'd awaken, tickle her out of bed, cook our breakfast, get her ready and drive her to school, kiss her, call out "See ya later!" And return home to climb back into bed where I'd mourn. Until time for me to drive back to school, take her to Brownies or piano lessons or gymnastics, cook our supper, help her with homework, bath, story, prayers. A kiss. And sleep.

Lost. I was lost in grief for years, and my little girl found me when I didn't realize I needed finding.

Saved. Love saves us all.

On Christopher's birthday last year, I began to journal about his adult self and the life he'd be living if death had not taken him so young. On paper, I imagined him as a farmer, as a good man who loved family and all of creation.

As I wrote details and imagined his life (and mine), I suddenly realized what I'd not included: his limitations!

I felt shocked that in those thirty minutes of writing, of dreaming a life with him still here, I never once remembered the reality of his disabilities.

If Christopher lived a fuller life span, he would have spent decades in wheelchairs.

Would he have better learned to eat, or still have a gastrostomy tube? Would he still have seizures daily?

Are there any medical advances to change how challenging his day-to-day existence would be? Would he live in a group home?

Why did I, for a few wonderfully delusional moments, imagine him as if he'd been born without all his physical challenges?

When he died, I wrote the poem that's on his tombstone and I suppose its words became my reality for him. To me, imagining him as a child without a wheelchair or seizure meds, brought just a little comfort.

I visit the cemetery and read these words carved onto the flat tombstone:

> The perfect angel he could be;
>
> Yet his little soul chooses
>
> Strong legs and arms
>
> Over angel wings.
>
> Flying can wait 'til another time
>
> While he runs, jumps,
>
> And dances by the sparkle of stars.
>
> He wants no halo,
>
> Rejoicing instead over candied apples,
>
> The flight of his kite to the rainbows,

And precious eyes that clearly see

Infinite sunrise and the smiles

Of each person he loves.

Already Heaven knows:

This is no ordinary angel.

Long, long after the shock subsided and the search for answers transformed into acceptance, grief's journey through guilt threatened my healing.

With both Christopher's and Jack's deaths, I was the person who spoke their life out of existence. The doctor talked to me about Christopher's lack of brain response and I gave my consent to remove the machines. The vet explained how Jack's tumor would continue to grow until more blood vessels burst, and I gave my consent to give the medicine to euthanize him.

What a heavy burden to bear when I began to realize I could have had another moment or another day, maybe even another week, with them.

I could have had Jack another day, maybe another few weeks if I would have waited.

I could have rocked Christopher one more time.

Grief will forever be a part of my life's journey. Once a woman I'd met only twice in social settings, but who knew about my son's death, commented to me, "I know a good grief counselor. You seem as if you always wear a cloak."

A cloak for my journey. I thought a lot about her words. I've worn this garment of mourning for 30 years as I write these words. I've decided I'll wear it always. Yes, on some days I feel its weight, heavy and dark. On other days, I fly with it like a super-shero's cape.

This morning I stood on the beach at sunrise. No matter how many times I see the horizon's spark turn into a blaze lighting the water, I still feel awed enough for tears to well up in my eyes and spill onto my cheeks.

When the moment was over, I turned and began to walk the shoreline. My pace was slow from pausing to look up at the waves and then down at the sand for shells. I noticed paw prints in the sand, but not the lopsided prints from the gait of a three-legged beagle. I sighed and stopped to search a stretch of beach where the tide had carried many shells to rest.

I heard a voice beside me, so close I startled a bit.

"What kind of shells are you trying to find?" the young man at my elbow asked.

"The pretty ones," I answered with a smile, "and they all are pretty to me."

"Do you want to find an olive shell?"

"Sure," I said, to be polite, unsure if I remembered how an olive shell looked.

""There's one!" He pointed to my right.

I looked closely for a few moments and then saw the only shell different from the rest. I picked it up.

He asked, "Is that an olive shell?"

I confessed, "It's been a long time since I've seen one, but I think so."

"Someone said that's what they're called," he said.

I held out the sea shell to him. "You spotted it, so you should keep it."

He beamed at me and said proudly, "It's for you."

I insisted with a smile, "You're so kind, but I want you to have it."

The young man accepted the shell, cradling it carefully in his outstretched hand. I heard a dog's bark behind us, so near that I turned in the other direction for a moment. The beach was empty. I turned back to the young man.

Christopher was nowhere to be seen.

Epilogue

In this world, my son, Christopher, never had a dog.

Christopher died ten months and ten days after we moved to the beach. He was almost seven years old when I rocked him for the last time.

In this world, my beagle, Jack, never had a boy.

Jack broke free from his chain 20 years after Christopher's death, and spent eight years as my beloved companion.

As Jack took his last breaths, I whispered words as true as any I know, "Your Boy is waiting for you. Run now, Jack! Run to your boy."

The Beagle is with his Boy now. And when I dream of heaven, I dream of that moment when I will see them both again.

Laughing and barking still, the boy's arms outstretched, his strong legs carrying him swiftly. The pup wagging, leaping, keeping pace beside the boy. They run closer and closer until my aching, reaching fingers touch my boy's hand, the beagle's paw.

And forever I am with them.

Acknowledgments

To readers who also have loved and grieved deeply, I hope these words bring some small measure of insight, hope, and comfort. My heart aches with yours.

This book's story is told through my lens about a deeply personal journey. I omitted most names of individuals and institutions for reasons of privacy and respect. Some names I'd prefer to shout for all the world to know of their goodness and positive difference in my journey. Other names are omitted with mercy and forgiveness. The names included, Clara and Mama Ree, belong to angels in heaven, where I'm certain they continue to love the beagle and his boy.

With my deepest gratitude and love, I acknowledge the following persons who made this book possible:

- Professionals and volunteers who dedicate their lives to the care and nurturing of children, especially those who treated Christopher with compassion and love.

- The saints who rescued Jack, especially his neighbor and the rescue's director, along with all those who give their hearts and resources to the rescue, fostering, training, and adoption of animals.

- Dr. Blake Peurifoy – a veterinarian whose heart's kindness matches his impressive professional skill, Paul Frye, and other friends at Cabarrus Animal Hospital.

- Jane Earnest, who welcomed Captain Jack's Library to the Family Care Center, and whose life's work makes our world a better place for all creatures.

- Those who shared their time and tremendous talents for the creation and publishing of this work, including Jessica Cook for editing and layout assistance; Paige Miles for drawing beagles, boys, and dragons; Anne Davis-Groebner for the book's cover art; and beta readers Stephanie Stergis, Monica Black, and Mike Kent.

- Friends who bring light and love into my life, and who offered encouragement and assistance, including Renae Leonhardt, Kathy Vestal, Paige Miles, Donna Rogers, Tam Wensil, Lynn MacDougall-Fleming, and Mary Ashley.

- Special thanks to my teachers, especially Miss Green from fifth grade and Sue Dennis, my favorite English teacher, and to Dr. Scott and Dr. Tamara for your guidance and kindness.

Last, and most, I thank my family for their constant love throughout my life's journey:

- My parents, Wayne Cook and Ann Garver Cook, who taught me I could be and do anything, because their belief in me never falters. Thank you, Daddy, for being the first person to encourage this story's telling, my hero cowboy and farmer, and the epitome of a loving father. Thank you, Momma, for rocking my children, being a feminist role model in your career path, and for your unconditional love.

- My siblings, Keith Cook and Kim Cook. I loved growing up with you, and treasure every moment with you and your families.

- Aunt Carolyn and Uncle Donald Brafford, for your inspiring courage this past year.

- Justin Woodell, for loving my little girl and for teaching me technology's most important lesson (turning it off and back on fixes almost anything!).

- Jessica, for your love and help with this book. You're the most incredible woman I know and still, always, you'll be my little girl.

- And to Ken, the love of my life, thank you for my morning coffee, for building me the most gorgeous library and writing desk any writer ever possessed, and for loving Jessica and me. I'm so thankful you came into our lives. Always, we'll *continue*! I love you!

Love to you all,

Cathy

Reader's Page

A Place to Remember Those You Love